To Billy —

I appreciate your feedback and I am enjoying my life outside the bar business. Best of everything.

Your friend,

Mike Shouse

Boomer Bungle

by

Mike Shouse

It does not take a BS degree in human studies (or any other BS for that matter) for an author to figure out who is most deserving of the thanks when it comes to the inspiration, patience, and support required to be the driving force behind the creativity in a writer. The question asked should be, "Is the author married?" Enough said. The spouse of a writer is that one person who carries the weight of mundane tasks, like having a real job that pays the mortgage, and explaining why her husband is holed up in his office writing again, instead of attending social functions. For every story I write, I am guided by an angel who provides me with the laughter and encouragement that keeps my passion alive... even in times when she might prefer to see my passion lying next to me in a coffin.

Patricia, I love you. I write for me... but I write because of you.

Contents

Contents cont'd

Preface, Preamble, Prologue...

Call it what you will. This is where I explain why I wrote what I wrote, and hold myself and this publisher harmless for damages, either to your sense of humor or your sense of self.

"BOOMER BUNGLE" is a 52-story, bi-weekly chronicle of a baby boomer's first stab at the game of retirement. It is a compilation of actual events that occurred as this author struggled to get a grasp on the emotional process of his maiden voyage into the post-working apocalypse. Some liberties were taken with minor details like truth and fact, but the stories are representative of the experiences we will all face as we age, I am sorry to say. It is part editorial, part journalistic (although actual writers may take issue with that), and often highly-hyphenated. It may be a guide for some, a set of rules for others, but most likely a warning to all: "Buckle up... retirement is not for the weak."

The working title for this book was "Boomer-Angst". The word 'boomer', derived from the Latin-like word 'boom' meaning big drive, references those individuals born between 1946 and 1964 who really like golf, and hitting the ball big off the first tee. And 'angst', derived from my Catholic vernacular, meaning those inescapable feelings of guilt and remorse. The combination represents the notion that, regardless of when we retire, the guilt of spending your time playing golf instead of contributing to society, is overwhelming and confusing. And like a boomerang, life has a strange way of coming back at you when you toss it aside, and will catch up with all of us someday.

But as you can see, that title did not survive the cut as there were already six other books with that exact name. Really, six? While none of those volumes have anything to do with my stories, I am a control freak with narcissistic overtones and identity issues... and I just wanted my very own title... okay? Thus, "BOOMER BUNGLE". It holds to the same premise as my original title, only my retirement anxiety is replaced by my inability to get it right the first time. Now I just don't feel guilty about it.

I have never thought of myself as an author, a writer of books. I like books; they look really cool all lined up in a row on the shelf. My office has floor-to-ceiling knotty hickory built-ins, chock full of the most popular 20th century titles. I just don't actually read them. I'm more of a short story man, and will never likely write a novel. Novels involve complex characters, around which a story line must be built, with a thickening of the plot, blah, blah. My attention-deficit tendencies have no patience for that discipline. Short, seemingly insignificant moments of day-to-day existence are the snippets of life that keep all things in perspective, and that's what you'll get from these stories.

As you make your way through retirement (and this book), be aware that your joys and your fears may both become amplified, probably because you realize the end is near. Remember, studies have shown that ten out of ten people die. It is my hope that you gain from my experiences or at least, take comfort in knowing others share the misery you are going through. In assembling this collection, it was not my intention to insult any one particular group or specific individual, but my hope to offend all equally. There is already too much hate in this world to single out the socially-inept and common sense-challenged idiots. Besides, you know who you are. There will always be rules to follow in the big game, but life is short, so don't take things too seriously. Have some fun reading this... and pay the fun forward...seriously.

Acknowledgements...And the Award Goes to...

Over the years I have had the great fortune to enjoy the company of many incredibly talented people who I count as friends. They make me feel as though I've hit the friendship lottery and I am grateful for their support, as they are always in my corner.

This page is for 'my team', who had a profound impact on the production of this book. To you I say, don't be discouraged by the fact that this page was originally supposed to be blank, but instead be discouraged that this is my only way of paying you for your efforts. While you are each deserving of the highest award for achievements in your category, I have no pretentious gold statuettes to hand to you. But true to Iowa hospitality, I can offer you an Isabel Bloom (cement) doorstop. That way, your door will always remain open so the fun people can wander in and out and help you keep your humor alive. My team:

Pat Shouse -   This is my awe-inspiring wife to whom I've already dedicated this entire book. What... you want more?

Linda Hurley –   Editor-extraordinaire (she'll have to look up how to spell that) and her husband Bob, for their guidance, punctuation, direction, and for keeping all my insecurities out of the way so I can continue to write... job-security strategy probably.

Amy Nielsen –   My illustrator. This is an artist who can draw your 'frame of mind' on paper and you'd swear your brain was looking in the mirror.   Thanks for the great pics.

Vicki Gray –   A person I've observed over the past few years who single-handedly inspires humor and creativity in others every day. Keep it up. Oh, and I may have stolen a quote or two from you.

"Thanks to my people... and of course... thank you Academy."

Boomer Bungle

Ignore the Question

OK, it is possible I may have been a little on edge earlier today, say around lunchtime. I was hungry and perhaps my blood sugar was a bit low. I did not go in to work today, or yesterday for that matter. Actually, I'm unemployed as of last Friday. The out-of-office reply on my email says: "Elvis has left the building". Yep, I am retired. Funny word R-E-T-I-R-E-D, like I just got another set of Michelins for my Jeep, or I was totally exhausted, but now I am exhausted again. I sort of like the sound of the word as it rolls off my tongue though, and I'm pretty sure I could get used to the concept of not ever working again... eventually, I think. A friend of mine called retirement "life's end-game", but surely death would hold that distinction. What do ya say we slow down and play the 4th quarter first?

My irritability actually began around 5:30 this morning. The barista was brewing the coffee I was desperate to get my hands on (the coffee, not the clerk), and she recognized me in line and shouted, "How's retirement?" Other customers turned to stare at me in anticipation of some witty response, but I drew a complete blank. Nobody had ever asked me that question before and I stood silent and red-faced. I grabbed the cup away from her, buried my face in the newspaper, and slinked out the door (yes, there was slinking). As I sat in my car I wondered about the curiosity others must have for this state of retirement. It must be a big deal... a milestone and a working stiff's ultimate goal ... but then what? I really don't feel or think differently at this moment. And I surmise this must surely be a process, a journey, the next chapter... but hopefully not the last chapter. So what do I say when asked the question? "I'm not working, but I'm working on it?"

In hindsight, I shouldn't have been surprised by the handshaking and congratulatory pats on the back when I walked through the bank later. They were one of the first to hear of the sale of our business. It was the teller who first formed the question: "How's retirement?" Then the vice-president, a loan officer, and the custodian chimed in. Absolutely nothing came out. My brain was firing on all cylinders but my mouth was slipping in-and-out of gear. I couldn't get my lips to form an answer and I became frustrated. That's not like me. The sound of the question suddenly made me feel old and wrinkly, and while that may be an accurate description of my physical attributes... I took offense today. I slipped out of the door without so much as a word, and the staff may have considered that to be a bit rude. Maybe I will use the drive-up on my next visit.

After a morning of texts and phone messages, I was looking forward to lunch with my beautiful wife, meeting at our favorite little deli across the street from the bank. This would be the perfect refuge from all the questions regarding my recent work status. We snuck into the corner booth that always seemed to be reserved just for us, and I felt calm and peaceful in that moment. But within seconds, the young waiter opened with, "How's retirement?" And before my wife could respond in the poised and graceful manner to which we are all accustomed from her, I blurted out, "Why don't you stick a sock in it, you millennial you!"

I had been mum all day, and when I finally got a response to come out, it was mean and vulgar. What's wrong with me? There was no call for that and I could tell I hurt his feelings. It is difficult for me to describe the look on this poor man's face when he crawled away from the table. The look on my wife's face however, was a familiar one I can describe all too well. I have seen that look on other occasions over our many years together, each resulting in my "retiring" to the couch come bedtime. Ever composed, my wife informed the waiter, "We're going to need that food wrapped up to-go if you don't mind". I am so in jail.

The first week of retirement has not been the warm and fuzzy journey I envisioned. I'm not convinced my wife will want to hang out with me all day on a regular basis either. I will have to come to terms with this new found arena I have tossed myself into, and get a plan together. Thankfully I have several options to choose from when I am next asked about my retirement thoughts. I can, (1) ignore the question all together and change the subject, (2) come up with a witty, standard response when asked, or (3) go back to work, making retirement a moot point. In that moment, my wife pushed the newspaper in front of me. I am sure it was just coincidence the 'Help Wanted' section was at the top of the pile.

Know Where You Are at All Times

They said it would happen... I scoffed. No way would the boredom of retirement ever take over our behavior, especially not in the first two weeks, and certainly not my wife. She is strong, determined, rock-solid, and perfectly sane. She had planned it all. We retired at the same time to seek out the endless adventures of our next life chapter, play golf, and relax by the pool sipping rum-soaked slurpies (say that three times really fast). But something is very wrong here. She's one of those gals that simply always has it together. I can't decide if she has lost her mind, or merely backed over it with the 4x4. Please tell me this is not happening.

I walked into the house today after 18 holes of golf and the mandatory 19th-hole cocktails that must follow every round. There she stood, sweatpants and ball cap, with her St. Ambrose Academy shirt tied off at the waist. She was sporting those long yellow gloves that Rubbermaid surely intended for nuclear waste removal, and she had that look in her eye. You know the one: "You don't measure up, scumbag. My mother told me about men like you. You've ruined my life." Yes, that one. My beautiful (and did I mention completely sane?) wife was positioned in our walk-in pantry dusting cans of Campbell's Soup we had probably purchased in college. There has always been soup in our house. We don't actually eat soup, but her mother is constantly warning us of the impending cold war invasion that will someday drive us into the cellar bunker she had built in 1960. Perhaps that could be a genetic clue I should have been more mindful of prior to today. She was slowly turning each red label towards the front, lining up the cans like little soldiers ready for the next dinner conflict.

She had been cleaning all day. You could smell the remnants of the battle between ammonia and bleach. Every dust bunny had been eliminated and every surface gleamed. I married Mr. Clean's sister so it was not surprising to see my wife picking up the house on a regular basis. But this was very different. There is 'company clean', where all the rooms on the main floor are spotless. Polite and proper company would not venture into unauthorized zones. It's like some sort of code women have. Then there is 'in-law clean', where everything gets a good going over, twice, and then my wife stops by Penney's to get a pair of new white gloves for the 'test'. Oh yes, trust me, there is an actual test. But today, oh my... the coats in the entry closet have been arranged by size and color. A jar of silver polish is on the counter. We have silver? I have entered a totally sterile and perhaps hostile environment. Tell me this is not happening.

I quickly get my bearings and realize I am still standing in the foyer, frozen in place. My keen senses alert me that tiny grains of sand are slipping out of the cuffs of my plaid pants and splashing loudly onto the travertine floor. I recall earlier events when I thought being in the sand trap would be the worst thing that would happen to me today. Silly me. Her stare is focused and intense. She is mumbling something. I slowly ease past her and duck into the den; I will be safe here. I am not alone; our two dogs are slumped against each other in the corner under the desk, shaking. I glance around to see all the books on the shelf have been alphabetized by author. What could have come over her today? I am getting an extra-terrestrial feeling about all this...and goose bumps. This sudden, obsessive-compulsive retirement persona is just temporary, right? Maybe I should seek professional help. I crawl to the desk and grab the Yellow Pages... c, d, e... there it is... "exorcist". Uh oh, I hear footsteps.

Get a Routine

There is a trick to this retirement thing, I'm sure of it. I am reminded of the street carnie running a shell game. It is nearly impossible to watch just one shell with the pea under it. This urban octopus moves and chatters at warp speed, all to throw off your concentration. The trick? Find the pattern of the hands in motion; don't focus on just one shell. There is a routine in place and if you ignore all the other distractions, you will experience the master plan. I have just described what must be the ideal program for anyone attempting retirement. This is not easy. Do not try this at home (move?).

Initially, it appears that the end-goal of any worker would simply be to stop working. That is the reward for 30+ years of hard labor. You paid your dues and it's time to quit. Adios, see-ya, bye-de-boo. But when the merry-go-round stops, or if you just hop off, the dizziness sets in. Your first instinct is to find the nearest cotton candy vendor or a Coney dog (it's getting close to my lunch time). "But twenty pounds later you realize that you are just fat and unemployed, and that is no way to go through life." I believe that is a direct quote from my wife; thus the need for some sort of a plan, a daily routine. That being said, please remember this is not an advice column. While I will gladly share my week-to-week experiences with you, I would not be your first choice for AARP poster child.

Establishing new routines, or changing old habits, is no walk-in-the-park for an old dog who is set in his ways. Once you stop going into the office, a fog sets in. I would equate the sensation to ramming your head through half-inch drywall. It looks fun when the Three Stooges do it, but a recent test of my theory reveals there is some pain involved. I might also note that the location of the 2x4 wall stud is a crucial element worth investigating, prior to the lunge forward. And be aware that paramedics apparently frown on treating self-inflicted head injuries, so there will be no sympathy offered for your pain. Take my word for this research. Once you wake up and realize there is no place you need to be, you have no incentive to engage the world. For the past three weeks I have been getting up every morning in order to do absolutely nothing all day, 24/7. I have a routine, it just consists of nothing. Remarkably, in that short period of time, I have been able to fully grasp the parameters of life as a slug. I stopped working, I stopped doing, and I totally dropped out. It is pitiful. Besides, my wife may not hang around much longer if I don't bathe soon. It is pretty clear that change is imminent and the need for a better routine is in my near future.

In a strange twist, my life as a worker seemed much simpler than my life as a retiree. The job had always dictated what I thought, when I ate, and who I socialized with. It's on me now; there's nobody else calling the shots... and it is frightening. I have become my own boss, and to be perfectly honest, I don't care much for my new employee. It is comforting to have my wife and dogs in the house with me, but they all seem to be giving me some space as of late... probably so I can find my routine.

So today is the day I will start my new plan. It's time for some discipline. I will make a master list of things to do including projects around the house, golf with friends, and romantic dinners with my wife (after the bath maybe). I will fill up the desk calendar with weekly goals, one step at a time. The possibilities of my newfound path are endless. I am very fortunate, this early in the game, to have figured out how important structure and planning are for a successful retirement. This week's list? I will carefully plan three morning golf dates, shave every other day, and work in a daily nap for each afternoon... with absolutely no distractions. Yes, this routine thing is working out splendidly.

Prepare for the Quiet

Where did everybody go? It's only been a month and I feel like I've slipped into a coma. The party they threw for us was a humdinger. Two hundred guests turned out to celebrate the selling of our business and leaving the workforce, though we might as well have left the country since we no longer hear from them. There were business associates, family members and friends from several states, co-workers, and former employees whose names I could not remember. We were blessed with countless toasts and roasts, and a tear-jerker video set to music. It was incredible. My wife went through a box of Kleenex, two hankies, and the right sleeve of my sport coat. Lots of great food, drinks, and memories were shared on the sun-drenched patio of our favorite Irish pub, and we enjoyed the perfect ending to our perfect careers. We are so lucky... and so alone.

I called the phone company this morning to see if crews were working in the area. Perhaps the service was interrupted for, say... four weeks? There have been no calls for power-lunches or 18-hole golf meetings during the week. Nobody calls with problems or dire situations that need my immediate attention. There's not one phone message checking on the status of anything. How do you get 'off' the national Do-Not-Call

List? Even our families wouldn't think to call during working hours, after all those years of never being at home. My wife & I had always worked, no exceptions. We gave up a lot of personal time to build and grow the business, and those closest to us suffered the consequences. All to make enough money to get to this very place in life. I didn't realize retirement was so... well, quiet.

For every high there is a low. I think that's Newton's Law. No, probably Murphy's Law, the Irish always have a way of rationalizing catastrophe. Can you remember leaving a concert or ballgame, and when you walked outside, the silence was deafening? That is exactly what retirement feels like at this stage. In the working years, we slowly ramped up the volume in our 'stereo of life', day by day, without noticing the decibel level. And now, it appears we have suddenly blown a woofer. The music has died... "Bye, Bye, Miss American Pie". I am only slightly terrified at this moment.

I guess it's the action I miss, or the interaction. I certainly don't miss the stress, but sort of miss the people who caused all that stress. Some people can put in the 8-hour day and drown their problems at the pub on the way home. Others can just flip off the switch. But my wife and I always brought the work home with us. We hashed over the events of the day and strategized over the challenges tomorrow might bring. It was our breath, our life fulfillment. But it all seems silly now. The work is never as important as the people you meet through work. And it would be really swell if any of those people would pick up the phone, as apparently the phone lines are now open. My only recent contact has been with 'Debbie' at the QVC Shopping Network. Funny how you can get to know somebody by only talking with them three or four times a day. Our mail carrier was usually good for a daily chat, but now with the extra packages being delivered, he just slows down and tosses the boxes onto the front lawn. Sure is quiet.

As I sit here and reminisce about that great party, a thought comes to mind. With all those nice people stopping by to share stories, filing by us one at a time, looking at the collage of pictures and the music video, I distinctly remember flowers and a priest. Wait a minute... is that why nobody calls anymore? "Hey honey, have you looked at the obits lately?" I need to go check my pulse.

Humility and the Fixed Income

The first thing I saw when I woke up this morning was my wife standing over the bed, eagerly waiting for my eyes to open and anxious to share the latest topic that kept her up all night. This was not an uncommon occurrence. In 26 years of marriage, she has rarely slept all the way through the night due to what she calls "mind-racing". And in the early years (and because I'm a guy), I envisioned stock cars going around a track inside her head and thought it must be kind of a cool experience. So you can imagine how disappointed I was to find out later that mind-racing was a bad thing.

On this day, and before I could ask what was up, she informed me it was my turn to get the groceries. Still in a sleepy stupor, I didn't fully comprehend the significance of her announcement, as was often the case. It has always been a pretty good ploy on her part to catch me early in the day with requests that push the envelope. The majority of me is up at 6:00 am, but that one lobe in my brain that provides me with the ability to say "no", doesn't get up 'til around 10:30. My wife first learned of this physical anomaly soon after we were married (like two days after the wedding). We still have that expensive antique hutch she bought on our honeymoon as a reminder.

I'm retired now, so how tough could one day of shopping be? Seeing no downside to this routine chore, and realizing the benefit of choosing my favorite snack items with which to fill the cart, I agreed. As my thoughts swam in pools of caramel and chocolate pudding, I was caught off-guard by the fact that she had not yet stopped talking "...and after 20 years of me always going to the store", she went on, "It's high time you took the next 20!" Did I just hear that the next 20 years would be my turn? What? I have just been tried, convicted, and sentenced to 20 years all before my Rice Krispies got soggy. Where is the number for my lawyer?

As I drove to the store, I was counting in my head the amount of cash I had on hand. I left my credit cards on the dresser and only grabbed my money clip on the way out the door, so anxiety was setting in. Forget the ATM, I couldn't tell you my pin number if you put a gun to my head (any robber reading this should keep that in mind). But surely $200 would take care of the list I was given and I'll be back home in time to catch the end of the golf tournament on TV. My wife was pretty specific about the brands of items to buy, especially when it came to the stack of coupons she stuffed into my shirt pocket. "Stick to the list. No extras! We are on a fixed income now." That means that our lives are governed by that pesky 6-letter word, b-u-d-g-e-t. I don't like that word. Actually, there are a lot of 6-letter words I don't like: bogeys, shanks, in-laws (oops). But this particular word implies we should live within our means, and that just seems so un-American. I was trying to keep a running total as I tossed each item into the cart, adding prices and subtracting the discount amounts... reminds me of my scorecard on the back-9 at the club yesterday. Did I bring enough money? What if I didn't? Fear is starting to set in.

This is truly one of those gender dilemmas. If women get all the way through check-out and don't have enough money, they simply tell the clerk to put three items back. Men on the other hand, would be too embarrassed for that. What if someone sees me? The universe would be all askew. Guys would explain that we left our wallet in the car, then go out and fish for quarters under the front seat to make up the difference. Or better yet, we'd flag down a perfect stranger and offer to sell him our watch. And in case there was any doubt, real men don't ask for directions either. We cannot admit we don't know what we're doing. Surprised? You are not.

The conveyor belt stopped and the register popped out the total... $198.92. YES! I did it! I handed the 4 fifty-dollar bills to the clerk and turned to high-five the mother of four in line behind me. "C'mon girl, get 'em up! No?" Awkward moment. This shopping excursion wasn't so bad after all. I can do this. I just need to remember the credit card next time. And let's see, I've only got 1,039 more until it's my wife's turn again. Maybe I should have gotten my lawyer involved.

White Lies or White Flags

I have just started my second month of retirement and I'm confused by so many unanswered questions. I would like to go play golf today, but it's 44 degrees and my first question is, "Why do I still live in the Midwest?" There must be lots of good answers to that one, but none come to mind right this second. I could go drown my links-withdrawal symptoms at my favorite Irish pub, but it doesn't open for 2 more hours. I believe we'd all greet the day better if Happy Hour ran from 7:00–9:00 a.m. Thus the second question, "Who makes liquor laws so restrictive?" Oh well, my wife has yet to appreciate my insistence that the sport of darts is good exercise, especially drunken darts. My cell phone keeps buzzing, but I know it's my neighbor wanting me to paint his recently-finished basement today. And that brings up perhaps the best question, "Why on earth would anyone in their right mind ever tell anybody they're retired?"

What was deafening silence during the first month of my unemployment has become criminal stalking of late. My handyman skills are in such high demand from friends and family, that I'm having trouble keeping everyone happy. Check that. I'm having trouble keeping me happy. I complained initially when my phone did not ring, and prayed I would not slip away unnoticed into the dark, retired night. Careful what you ask for. It seemed nobody called to ask for anything when I had the time, and now... anybody calls all the time to ask for everything. I feel like the only customer service rep at an international call center. I haven't heard from this many friends since I owned a pickup truck.

I'm not sure why family members are especially under the assumption that being retired means having absolutely nothing to do. Okay, while possibly correct, it is still my time to waste and not their void to fill. I don't want to spend my days crossing off items on their honey-do lists. My wife's sister says, "Poor guy, sitting around in that hammock every day, all bored and unshaven... he needs me to find a project to keep him busy." Bless her little heart. I'm not tiling her kitchen, no matter how concerned she is for my well-being. Either learn to say "no" or kiss your spare time bye-dee-boo. Or... stretch the truth far enough to bend it all out of whack, but remain intact (sort of). It's not really like lying (okay, that's not true). It is semantics: A linguistic arrangement that says what you mean without meaning what you say. For instance: "I can't tell you how sorry I am that I did not call you back." Translated: You didn't call and you aren't sorry, and that's why you can't tell them. Or, "I'm sorry. I wish circumstances had been different last Friday when you asked me to clean out your gutters." You were actually playing golf badly that day, and you wish you had played better (thus your sorrow), but there was never an intent to do anything other than play golf. It is nearly impossible for me to lie to my wife's family. Somehow I manage.

If you can't bring yourself to lie, then you'll have to put some stories in place that perpetuate an on-going truth. Stop by your old office and call your cell phone. Then when asked to remodel a bathroom, just say the office called and you went to work. Both statements are true. Or, drive to the next town. When asked why you couldn't help move that couch up to the attic, you tell them you were out of town. And you truly were... at some point. Whatever your plan, there is one rule you must always adhere to. Never, regardless of the circumstances, answer your door or home phone during the day. You are just asking for trouble. Better yet, have the machine tell callers to leave a message after the beep... then erase the beep. I'm pretty sure my neighbor is still on hold from his call last Tuesday. And always hold your cell phone out the window of your car, so callers will think you are too far away to stop by and look at their leaking toilet. Sounds silly, but it works. Stand your ground (preferably a fairway somewhere in Florida), or suffer the consequences. Be proactive and stay alert. "Was that the phone? No honey... don't answer that!"

Take the Fork in the Road

My wife informed me over coffee one morning that she wanted to "see the USA in our Chevrolet" and we would be taking the back roads to Daytona. At first, I thought we were headed to the 'big race', but that's not for another six months. I told her about AirTran's 2-4-1 flight specials, and suggested flying would be much better, right? She said we were driving. We don't own a Chevrolet. I can't remember the last time my wife and I 'drove' to Florida. Why would anyone trek 1200 miles at 55 miles per hour when every airline offers four flights a day? Driving is certainly not cheaper, what with the price of gas and hotels. Factor in the fatigue of a three-day drive down state roads, and three days back on county roads... where did the week go? And don't forget about 'Jetta-lag' in our Volkswagen. Your asking me if this a good idea? Don't rush me, I'm thinking. I like vacations, but this trip to see back-door America isn't one of my bucket-list items. I knew watching that rerun of "On the Road with Charles Kuralt" the other night, was a bad idea. At least she didn't rent a motor home... or a film crew. We might not want to replay the video of us cooped up in a vehicle for a week. So we are about to "head south, take in the sights, and spend time with family members who live along the route." Family? Who said anything about family?

Whoa, Nelly!   I haven't seen my two cousins who live in Memphis since I was twelve. I remember distinctly because 12 was also their I.Q. We have never been close and I'm not sure which branch of the family tree my wife shook, to get those names to fall out. She has never met them or their spouses... or their children, who are likely flunking out of high school right about now. She is under the impression that reaching out to them will 'complete' our lives somehow. Couldn't we just write a postcard in Florida and drop it in a mailbox? Surely they get mail in Tennessee. And then we're off to see my 'Uncle Carl' in Georgia? You're killing me here. If we go to his house we're going to have to take a case of beer. For that matter, we'll need to drink a case of beer before we get there. I'm not sure I can talk politics for a whole evening... at least not his politics. And why did you agree to stay overnight at their houses? Are there no hotels south of the Mason-Dixon Line? This will not be a trip down memory lane, but more like a stumble down disappointment alley.

I tried to pass the drive time with memories of similar trips with my grandmother when I was a kid. She had this Corvair convertible and we cruised from town to town, hitting every Stuckey's on the route to Tampa. I loved Stuckey's praline logs and would spend hours going through their gift shops. It was a blast. There were few interstate roads back then, and with the top down, we could experience all the sights and smells of small-town America. We sang songs and played the 'license plate game', and summer vacations with Memaw were the best! On this trip all I smell is burnt diesel fuel and half a burrito that got wedged under the front seat last week. I have yet to see a Stuckey's. And if I had a top to drop, the pouring rain wouldn't allow it. This is no blast.

We made the first stop in Memphis and unfortunately my cousin remembered we were coming. After a delicious dinner and some small talk, we all moved to the family room to reminisce about days gone by. The conversation got around to the time 'Duane' got locked in the boathouse and somebody started a small fire outside the door to make him cry. I laughed so hard I thought I was going to pee my pants. By the time I realized nobody else was laughing, it was too late. Busted. With all the commotion from the fire trucks that day, nobody knew who set the fire. And had we not stopped to visit family on this trip, they would never have known it was me. Within seconds after that story, my wife started yawning and checking her watch. We all hit the sack rather early, but it took me a while to double check all the door and window locks in our guest room. And I didn't get much sleep, being up most of the night testing the batteries in the smoke alarm. In hindsight, sneaking out before breakfast might have been a bit rude, but a good call nonetheless. We pushed the car out of the driveway and were off.

As we left Tennessee, the rain was still hammering us. Sirius Satellite Radio was forecasting hurricanes for the east coast, not sunshine over the next few days. At this point I am still excited in anticipation of white sand beaches and lush green golf courses, but hope is fading. With a few hundred miles between us and 'Duane', I started dreading our next stop. Uncle Carl had lost his wife a few years ago and was on a mission to find other women to replace her: Stella Artois, Skinny Blonde Ale, and St. Pauli Girl. Beer had become his life. When we knocked on the door he hadn't remembered that we made plans to visit him. The gift of beer was likely his second case of the day, and I doubt that either of us remembers much of our brief conversation. My wife was finally realizing the magnitude of her decision to descend on distant relatives. She cancelled all other travel plans to see family, and we headed directly for the Sunshine State.

I was briefly excited to see the Florida Welcome Center's sign for free orange juice as we approached the exit. Looking over the map while sipping the lukewarm, pulp-free, low-carb, orange flavored drink from a recycled cup, you could see the remnants of the recent storms. Our hotel on the beach sported a blue tarp over its roof. The management assured us the cracks in our suite walls were not structural. Buckets were collecting water in the dining room. The debris scattered along the entire eastern coastline covered up any sand, white or otherwise. The National Hurricane Center had just assigned the last of the alphabet names and the rain was still pounding. This was a record year for hurricanes and there would be no golf, no swimming, and no fun on this trip.

The 22 hour drive back, via interstate highways, was quiet and there was no singing. This was not the journey my wife had been looking forward to, and I am glad we are finally home. In hind-sight I probably shouldn't have bought the tee shirt that reads, "Up Your Chevrolet, See the USA in a Ford", but it was two-for-one. She has not tried hers on yet. The clamor of pots and pans from the kitchen reminds me that somehow this bad road trip is going to end up my fault, so I'd better get prepared. I'm dialing... "Hello? 1-800-FLOWERS?" Help is on its way.

Searching, Not Hunting

I can attest to the struggles associated with finding hobbies to fill the hours of a retiree's day. The time that's left over after you sleep for six hours (if you're lucky), and eat for six hours (if you're very lucky and live next to an ice cream shop), is twelve hours. That's 84 hours a week you need to be doing something besides eating and sleeping. Go ahead, try to come up with a list of projects that will take up your next 4,368 available hours in the coming year. My wife suggested volunteering. Four thousand hours? If I showed up at the soup kitchen that often, the homeless would have me arrested for stalking. And I really should be thinking of something more fun than being jailed.

Because I'm an avid golfer, I was sure the answer was hitting the links every day. Avid does not necessarily translate into 'good'. But I tried that for a few months and couldn't get my spine to fully cooperate with the rest of my flailing appendages. I actually got worse with more play, and it was not pretty. In summary, I was either too sore to play, or played too bad and was sore (at my game). A hobby should be fun. My conundrum encouraged me to consider other possible pursuits and I sought help from the internet. Turns out, the top five hobbies for retired men are, in order: 1- Fishing, 2- Golf, 3- Woodworking, 4- Not answering your neighbors' calls... and, 5- Hunting.

Forget number one, I don't fish. I've found absolutely nothing wrong with the frozen fillets you can buy at the grocery store and they don't smell up the truck. I may be jaded by that one fishing experience, wherein I left a large-mouth bass under my front seat for a few days, and whenever I turned on the A/C, my lips puckered and I got blue in the gills. Golf may be ranked second, and I so love the game, but I'm just no good at it. As for number three, I like woodworking and own practically every power tool ever made. I've enjoyed a variety of projects over the years, even the ones I was talked into for my neighbors. I believe that pretty much sums up my feelings about hobby number four. As for hunting, I was somewhat surprised. I was unaware that so many Americans were enamored with shooting harmless, unarmed animals for sport. I have guns around the house, and fully support the NRA and the 2nd Amendment, but those are for protection. I only hunt when I'm walking down the grocery aisles looking for the frozen fish department.

My wife takes on an entirely new persona when defending the rights of the 'small & furry'. She despises those who hunt, referring to them as "bearded, camouflage-clad cowards who wake up on weekends with a hangover, just looking for some defenseless creature to take it out on." She kinda has that whole 'poor Bambi' thing going on and could benefit from a wee bit of therapy, if you ask me. But she is entitled to her opinion, and even if she wasn't, no gun-totin' yahoo is going to get in her way.

Shortly after we were married, we moved out to the beauty of the country (probably to escape the gunfire of the city). We were never near any of the drive-by shootings that too often make the news, but what little private time we had outside of work, we didn't want spent amidst the sights and sounds of urban life. Instead it seems, we traded for the gunfire of the country. The woods behind our house border a cornfield and provide the ideal cover for deer and pheasant and other wild critters trying to dodge the bullets of those "morally-bankrupt murderers". My wife has a long list of names for the hunters who wisely stay the required 200 yards from our house. While she may despise hunting, she's a pretty good shot and knows her way around guns.

Whenever we hear the first crack of gunfire just before sunrise, my wife races to bring the dogs in, and goes immediately into G.I. Jane mode. She whips out the five-million candlepower flashlight (this baby lights up most of the county), and grabs her megaphone. That's right... she has a megaphone. She barks out her opinions to those who are hell-bent on destroying the family unit of the goose gaggle. Canadian geese are always in route from a neighboring pond straight to ours. I have spent many Saturday mornings crouched behind our wood pile, listening to my wife yell at the hunters who blast away at the unsuspecting flock overhead. After scores of unresolved calls to the Department of Natural Resources and the sheriff, she has decided to take matters into her own hands, or should I say... my hands. She read an article about a scientist's experiment to re-train the flight patterns of migratory birds. And that got her thinking. While I doubt the scientific community would endorse her theory, her efforts should at least be published in a journal. Oh wait, I just did that. My next woodworking assignment would become a 30-foot long, 8-foot wide, red & yellow plywood arrow. Seen from the sky, it is designed to warn the geese of impending doom, and safely divert their path around our woods. I am anxious to see how my wife is going to teach these geese the significance of this arrow. According to her, "It'll be a lot easier to educate the bird than the bird-brained." I certainly married one tough bird.

Age Has Its Privileges

Since retiring, I've noticed that age comes with certain perks. I appreciate the respect that is earned by those who have paved the way before us, and fully support America's recognition of our elderly. But at 57, I do not believe I fall into the 'senior' category, though I've got a nephew who has me only three shovels of dirt away from my final resting spot. So I wonder who decided to label anyone near 60 years old, a 'Senior Citizen'? Sixty? That's still spring-chicken territory, my friend. And step back or I'll open up a can of 'Whoop-Ass' and come straight at you. Like it or not, it is apparent that society suggests that once you get an AARP card and two gray hairs... you should be entitled to a mother-load of discounts.

I don't remember the first time it happened. People are now offering to get things down off of high shelves for me. I still remember how to operate a ladder. I am also asked to move ahead of others in line at the grocery. What? Are they concerned I won't live long enough to finish grilling the T-bone I just bought? Nice, but unnecessary. Discounts are now available to me on just about everything I buy. And while it's great to save money, I don't get the marketing strategy. If managers are in search of customer loyalty, am I really considered a long-term candidate? And if I am, it's likely I won't have enough money left over after medical bills to go anywhere. I can only assume the original senior discounts first began when the average life expectancy was much lower, and old people were not seen as a long-term threat.

But age-discriminating specials are unlike other discounts. If you are a military veteran, you are being recognized for your contribution. Soldiers fought for our country and their families made sacrifices. Yes, by all means they deserve a discount. But me? I get to pay less just because I haven't died yet? I don't get it. And is it politeness that inspires younger people to open doors for men my age... or pity? "Yes, let's get that door for him. See that gray hair? He is likely on his way to visit his lawyer to get his affairs in order."

Look, I'll take the 10% off, the vacation upgrades, and the moves to the head of the lines (I like getting home before my ice cream melts), but you've got to let me open my own door, OK? If you see me struggling with a door, just push me to the ground and walk over me. I should not be out in public trying to go through doors I can't open. Maybe it's just a gender fault, a 'guy thing'. My wife says we men have a lot of those. Growing up, I was taught to open doors for women of any age, young children, and the elderly. Maybe that's the rub. I am considered by some to be an elder adult now (my wife would probably question the 'adult' part). Could my life have zipped along that quickly? I don't think I'll ever get used to it.

Women and doors have a whole different relationship, though. Girls get doors held for them from the time they start walking. Cordial? Perhaps; but more likely it's a man opening the door thinking, "She's only nine now, but in ten years she'll be in college and we can go out together." Creepy, huh? My wife says this chivalrous act demonstrates kindness and that women like it. To have a door opened is not a sign of aging for women because they're used to it happening their whole life. That may be why emergency rooms in this country see 10,000 cases of forehead injuries every year; all women who reported doors that were not open at the time of their attempts to enter. In complete contrast, there are absolutely no reports of this medical phenomenon occurring for men. Things that make you go...hmmm.

While I may not be accustomed to some of the perks of aging, let me be very clear about the early-bird dinner specials. These restaurant people are geniuses! They were never serving any meals between 4:00 and 5:00 p.m. prior to this revelation. And while the price is discounted, the margin of profit per entrée is enough to cover the labor of the kitchen staff that had to come in early to prep anyway. Us 'old folks' are always out of there in plenty of time to turn-over the tables for the normal dinner crowd, 'cause there's no way in hell we'd ever miss an episode of Wheel of Fortune; truly a win-win.

We all have to try not to take any of this aging thing too seriously. You are born, you grow up, and then you buy-one-get-one free. It's the cycle of life, and who am I to try to fool with Mother Nature. The process of aging is just fine like it is. It's when that process comes to a halt, that the seriousness becomes grave... literally.

Togetherness Is Key

Don't get me wrong, I love my wife. We have one of those great relationships where we are best friends, soul mates if you will, and that bond has gotten stronger with every year of marriage. We like the same movies, agree with the same politics, and crave the competition of playing golf against each other (unless she beats me). We were successful partners in business, working side-by-side, and retired at the same time so we could focus on this next life chapter together, t-o-g-e-t-h-e-r, as in not apart.

Where did she go? It's been two months now. After friends threw us a swell retirement party, and we re-connected with some family members across several states (there's 9 days, 3 hours, and 6 minutes she owes me big for), we cleaned out the garage and tackled a house project or two, and then POOF! She vanished. I never see her anymore. She's off today with this band of seven women who go shopping, lunching, golfing, and other gang-related activities. They are inseparable. It's pathetic.

This group of good-time gals has been friends since grade school. They all grew up in the same small town, worked together off and on in various jobs over the years, and shared teenage girl-drama throughout high school. They have a lot in common. Each got married, then unmarried, and re-married all about the same times. Each left that small town for a brief period, but returned. There have been birthdays and funerals and graduations all intertwined, with what one must admit is true friendship. And during our working years, I remember us squeezing in occasional dinners out with the husbands, though none of us are best friends. Besides, guys don't have friends like that. With a few exceptions, our friend is the guy we just sat next to at the bar, engaged in an hour of inebriated sports trivia. Not really life-long buddies, more like day-long pals.

I'm not the clingy type. I honestly like my space and I'm glad she has friends to hang out with. But this morning, as my face was being licked by our dogs (they each have their own unique breath, by the way), she crossed the line. I reached over to nudge my wife, who always takes the morning shift with the dogs, and read the note on the bedside table: "The girls decided on a last-minute trip to the Mall of America. Go ahead and eat dinner without me." Dinner? What about breakfast and lunch? This is not short notice, this is no notice. The mall is in Minneapolis. We don't even live in the state of Minnesota. I'm guessing she may be home a tad late. Two weeks ago, they all took a 3-day golf junket to Myrtle Beach. The week before that, they flew to New York to appear on the Today show plaza. In her defense, I did actually get to see her on that day as Al Roker stopped to comment on their pink hats. How cute.

I'm OK with take-out food, computer solitaire, and walking the dogs, but I do not think this behavior is normal. When all together, these grown women goo-goo and gah-gah like 8-year olds at a sleepover. My wife says they laugh so hard, sometimes there is the dreaded "peeing of the pants". That is just

not right. Men over 50 don't have fun like that. We get grump-
ier, I'm told. Probably because we wet our pants and don't
find it that funny. Crisis in mid-life affects us all differently, I
suppose.

With an unexpected day to myself (again), I think I'll call up
some friends and go to the shooting range. No, maybe grumpy
old men wielding weapons with live ammunition is not such a
hot idea. Well, golf then? Same problem, the hackers I play
with wouldn't be much safer. I guess I'll just take the dogs for
another long walk. They don't mind being out in this weather.
"Come on kids, let's go outside again." Grrrrr... how tough is it
to get somebody out of a gang?

Habits Aren't Just for Nuns Anymore

I make the bed every morning. My wife is always up early with the dogs and allows me an extra wink or two. But page three, paragraph one of the marriage manual states unequivocally, that the last person to touch the bed has to make it. Marriage is nothing without rules. As I am pulling up the blankets on my wife's side of the bed, I always find a pair of socks stuffed under her pillow. She goes to sleep with socks on, but at some point in the night she removes them and slips them under her pillow. Why would anyone do that? I have asked her many times over the years to explain the logic in this habit, and her response is consistent, "I've just always done it". Well, there you go then. I believe that it stems from her poor childhood and a fear that the sock-monkey might steal her knitted ninnies. That would constitute a 'hose heist', and I can think of nothing scarier than that, honey. Yes, of course I'm making fun of you. If the Easter bunny was somehow involved, it would explain why you never attended any sock-hops in high school. I will remain alert, but it is not likely I will fall prey to this rash of suspected burglaries. The last place I'd want to put my socks after a long day is under my pillow... at least not if I wanted to get any sleep.

After the age of about fifty, most of us have spent more time married than single. For whatever reasons you chose to go that route in the beginning, it's the subsequent training and instruction (pay attention husbands) that ultimately keeps the two of you together. Wedded bliss? Only if you follow a few simple rules. Take those little idiosyncrasies that you thought were so adorable during the dating period. These can eventually become annoying habits as the years pass. And when those habits become 'disgusting', spouses often weigh the advantages of homicide (and fifteen years in prison) over tolerance. The key to a good marriage, especially in your retirement years when you spend "sooooo much time together" (a direct quote from my wife), is acceptance. Learn to look past the trivial junk through the periods of "to have and to hold", to "behave and be told", all the way to "be glad that you're old". Let it go. Only an idiot would harp on these insignificant peeves and print a list of them for others to see. So as not to disappoint, this idiot continues.

My wife and I share the laundry duties and there always seems to be a load ready to move from the washer to the dryer. She has this habit of stuffing the washer as if our well is going to run dry and there will be no more water after this next cycle. "Last chance dirty clothes... all aboard!" Whatever the manufacturer recommends as a maximum capacity for this machine, she 'super-sizes' it. I have explained that the stress on the motor will shorten its life expectancy. And in order to get really clean, a certain amount of room in the drum is necessary to allow the clothes to move against each other in an agitating fashion. Apparently my suggestion alone is agitation enough for her. The dryer succumbs to the same fate as it was not designed to dry 42 wet towels per load. We have put down seven washer/dryer sets in our married existence.

I like that our house is always clean. But my wife will follow me around and pick-up, and re-straighten, and set a coaster under my glass before it hits the table. She is a nut about vacuuming and often leaves the Dyson running, just in case dust might be thinking about hitting the floor soon. I can't leave a dish in the sink or my keys on the counter when I get home. There is a place for everything and everything must be in its place. She makes tomorrow's coffee and sets the timer before today's pot even gets cold. It is cute and endearing... at times. But, I take it all in stride and I'm thankful she will never write a book and tell the world about my quirky habits.

I tease my wife about her eccentricities, few and minor as they are. She takes the kidding in stride and we maintain our marital balance. Sharing little quips about her odd characteristics might be fun in moderation, but I should stop now and take care not to recite a long list. That could shorten my life expectancy and I might go the way of our past washing machines. My wife does not snore, chew with her mouth open, or smoke cigars. She has absolutely no disgusting habits. She does not interrupt when I talk or repeat gossip about anyone. She is a kind and wonderful person. And upon reflection, her aforementioned habits are certainly not character flaws and really don't annoy me. To be completely honest, my wife is perfect. Well there you go. Can you think of anything more annoying than that?

Be Happy

From the deck I can just see the sun popping up across the empty cornfield. It is by far the coldest morning yet of the fall season. I suppose the temperature is hovering in the mid-forties, so I would be generous using the word 'brisk'. The striking white lines in the sky mark the early morning jet trails and a handful of wispy clouds frame the otherwise blue picture. It is calm and perfect. As I slip out of my robe and quickly submerge into the steaming bubbles of the hot tub, I draw a huge breath as the water engulfs me. The splash startles a nearby rabbit in the bushes. The hum of the Jacuzzi motor provides a music track for the low cackle of a Canadian goose on the pond across the creek. There is nothing better for these old bones than the therapy jets aimed at my joints. And there is nothing better for this old spirit than the still and quiet of the Midwest countryside at dawn. I am blessed to have found this moment in time and I have caught myself grinning... I am relaxed, and happy.

I also feel a bit guilty. I do not have to go to work today. I am enjoying the fruits of my early retirement. I was so fortunate to have sold my business at a good time, and while I may not be retired forever with this failing economy, I am certainly cherishing this peaceful respite. I am glad to be unemployed. I rarely had much time for hot tubs or hot times during my working years. I loved my work but it consumed me. My wife and I were always so busy and we missed out on so many little pleasures. Don't get me wrong, there have been moments of happiness in my life. Admittedly, I did have to look harder sometimes to find them. With so many obstacles in the way, we can all have trouble at times seeing the forest because of the trees. I am often reminded that there will be disappointments and failures on our journey, but the measure of one's success should be in how you respond to adversity, not in how you try to avoid it. Pretty heavy stuff for so early in the day, huh? Life is good and I am in a good place.

The ringing phone blares like a trumpet amid all this serenity. I have no idea who would call so early, but I welcome the coffee my wife brings along with the cordless handset. Regardless of the intruder, nothing could possibly spoil the purity of

this experience. I immediately recognize the voice as my neighbor who lives on the other side of the pond. He has a higher pitched tone than normal and is hurried in his attempt to get his message out, almost yelling I sense. I catch a few jumbled phrases that sound like, "Why don't you put some clothes on!" and "exposing yourself to my wife is against the law in this state!" Did he just call me a pervert? I was naked for all of 3 seconds before hopping into the water. Besides, they live 400 yards to the west and even with binoculars (which I'm sure Gladys has), the imposing sun would distort any details other than a faint human outline. That woman has quite the imagination and may have needs that are not being met. I doubt that a reply to this rant would be a good idea right now. And my guess is he's just jealous of my newfound retirement, poor working stiff. I will respond to this adversity by winking at his wife at the next block party. Ah...once again I am happy.

The Grass Is Always Greener

The plans arrived in the mail today. My goodness, there must be a dozen or so from every state south of the Mason-Dixon Line. The internet is truly an amazing thing to behold (thank you, Mr. Gore). One day you're totally bored, double-clicking on 'golf get-aways' and 'golf home sites', dreaming of warm winter climates. And the next day you're fixing your mailbox, broken under the weight of some 200 packets of prospective new retirement communities that the mailman begrudgingly stuffed in. Actually, there was a paper trail all the way to the neighbor's fence (reminder: no Christmas tip for the postal worker this year). There are so many choices of floor plans and construction styles, if we just took the time to go over all the material, we'd spend our golden years reading our way through retirement. Every brochure shows plush fairways and fabulous pools. They are each offering free stays and huge discounts on lots. "Get 'em while they last!" We decided to toss out every state except Florida and Arizona, with apologies to all those other fine destination states.

Those of us who spent our first 50 years stuck in the frozen tundra of the Heartland are sitting ducks for the marketing wizards at retirement communities. Maybe sucker is a better word. Our six months of green-grass time is spent mowing and trimming, followed by cursing and weeding. The other six months is spent wishing for green-grass time. If you guessed that today was December 5th, and that I woke up to 8 inches of fresh snow this morning, you'd be a good guesser. How'd you do that?

So when a marketing brochure, full of pretty pictures and unbelievable promises, gets delivered directly to our door... we pay strict attention and assume the stars have aligned to chart our tropical path. There is a logical reason for the two states that we picked for potential retirement homes. Each has 300 days of sunshine annually, an average temperature of 70 degrees, and is home to hundreds of the world's best golf courses. The fact that they are at the far ends of this big country of ours and would require a considerable amount of effort on the part of friends and family to visit regularly, is purely coincidence.

As we read the fine print and went gah-gah over the pristine beauty of each catalog, I struggled with the continued reference to the term, "active adult community". Are there 'inactive' communities for sale? I suppose cemeteries fall into that category. The cost of a plot per square foot is about the same, but with the casket you wouldn't have to shell out property taxes or insurance. And you wouldn't need a coat of paint every 15 years either. They offer a fine looking 'Colorado Pine' model. My wife fails to see my humor. The real kicker in these pamphlets appears to be "common area maintenance" fees. Beware! Those monthly C.A.M. dues are steep, and for $350/month... I'm sure my wife is going to expect a maid, a gardener, and a pool boy. It's as if you are buying the lot, paying to build a house, and then renting the view for the rest of your life; ridiculous, but popular.

I notice that every brochure touts their commune as gated and guarded. I'm not sure if the walls are there to keep others out or you in. But, security appears to be a huge selling point at these places. Armed patrols go around 24 hours a day. Really? Did the developer get a good deal on the land because it's in a bad part of town? I suppose making newcomers feel safe is good marketing. If you've been married as long as I have, you probably don't want your own loaded gun in the house any-way...especially knowing your wife's genetic predisposition for Alzheimer's.

"Hey honey, I'm home from the golf course."

"Who are you and why are you in my house?" BANG!

It's no wonder more people die in retirement than any other period of their life.

Double Your Bubble

We live in a country that is likely the all-time greatest melting pot in the world. And retirees from each state have ventured to Florida throughout the years to unite to become this huge collection of 'fun' thinkers. With every decade that passes, a new generation of settlers has come here with plans saying," If I ever get the chance to create my own utopia, this is how I would do it." I am in awe. Residents banding together, insisting on cheap golf played on beautifully manicured courses, an abundance of good restaurants with inexpensive food (they invented the early-bird dining experience), and places where streets encourage golf carts over gas-guzzlers. Throw in the backdrop of an ocean bordered by white sand beaches, and the gorgeous sunsets are simply a bonus. You couldn't script retirement any better; unless of course, you mixed it with alcohol.

One of the first age-restricted golf communities we looked into was in central Florida. We were interested in adult communities (55-and-over) for the obvious reason... no kids. My wife and I are not anti-children; we are just anti-your-children. Grandkids can change the complexion of a swimming pool, not to mention the color. All that splashing and screaming and having fun, only reminds old people how young we aren't. I could live with a rule where residents can only be blessed by visits from their offspring three times a year, with a maximum of two weeks at a time. This particular oasis boasted 50,000 homes on six gazillion acres and offered free golf on its executive courses for life. I assume they meant my life, but you always want to put the magnifiers on when reading fine print.

After touring the grounds by shuttle (which took most of the day), we were herded into a room for a video presentation that would explain prices, options, and upgrades. It was not the marketing department's first rodeo. The layout of the golf courses was spectacular. The homes were gorgeous and grouped around 'town squares', each created to replicate Small Town, USA from yesteryear. Every home had a front porch with a rocker. Sidewalks were wide and invited after-dinner walks to get out and meet your neighbors. It all had this warm & fuzzy ambience and you could smell grandma's apple pies cooling on the window sill. "Take all the time you need, we are not a high-pressure sales group. Pick up your complimentary hat and sunglasses on your way out to visit the main town square this afternoon, and we'll be here when you come back to sign you up for your new address." The hook was set.

We could hear the country-western band as we stepped out into the humid air. There had been a brief shower while we were inside getting our brains washed. They were kicking off the start of 'Happy Hour on the Commons', a four-hour-long block party that started every day at 3:00 pm. Every day? As we came closer to the square, we were greeted by thousands of golf carts lined up in their little parking spots, each as unique as their owners, I'm sure. There were people dancing and I dodged them on the way to one of the twelve bars that were set up. I ordered two gin and tonics and was given four. Oh yeah, double-bubble no less. A five dollar bill covered the cost and I was handed a tray to make my walk back through the crowd easier. I'm a big fan of outrageous service so I was pretty darned impressed with the promise of this new lifestyle.

After the party ended, when we might have been tempted to head back over to the sales office and sign on the dotted line, we witnessed 'the spectacle'. In all their inebriated glory, thousands of weaving carts took off at once, racing home to catch 'Jeopardy' on TV. Jeopardy is exactly what we felt like we'd be in, if we were to buy a house in this place. There were no signs of security, and public decorum had pretty much been tossed out with the ice cubes. It seemed to us that this easy-going lifestyle would be punctuated every day by dodging intoxicated, aggressive drivers at sunset. A house in the median of the Florida Turnpike might be safer. The hat and dark glasses came in handy as we snuck by the sales office on our way to the front gate.

The Big Move

The decision to move to Florida was mostly mine, according to any reports my wife gives out to others. We had vacationed both there and in Arizona on numerous occasions, and felt comfortable with the amenities and weather in either state. But most recently, a few good friends had retired to the Orlando area and we shared the same passion for golf and more golf. So we pored over many great house plans and picked one to build in one of those gated golf communities and the completion date was nearing. After contacting a few moving companies and finding their prices to be the equivalent of three years worth of greens fees, I hinted to my wife that we could move ourselves. Thoughts of tooling down I-75 with our bedroom strapped to a flatbed truck like Granny Clampett must not have appealed to her. That made me think of Ellie Mae in those cut-off jean shorts, but what I said aloud was, "U-Haul". I believe wives sometimes give in to their husbands rather than try to explain the stupidity of the male thought process. Too exhausting, I suppose. Her only comment was, "You'll have to find another driver. The dogs and I will be taking the Chrysler." Okay, I can do this! I love a challenge.

Calculating the cubic feet capacity for the contents of two trucks was simple, compared to deciding what personal items to take with us and which ones to give away. Will she pick the dining room hutch or the antique end table? No dear, they both won't fit. It can be humbling (not to mention dangerous) trying to reduce your married net worth down to two box-trucks. My sister-in-law now owns that end table. And I am surprised to this day that I wake up every morning without a pair of scissors sticking out of my chest. My wife loved that antique and hasn't forgiven me yet.

I was about to haul the balance of our life's treasures across six states and I needed a second driver. Good luck with that. A big, bulky rental truck would not be easy to maneuver through major-city traffic, and the comfort level would be basic at best. With only a week to go and no takers for helping me, I was at a party and overheard a friend telling of his plans to take a few work days off to fish and play some golf. I called 'Stan' the next day to see if his time off from work coincided with my travel plans. I think he was caught off guard by my request, and I attribute his saying "yes" to a huge hangover and a desire to get me off the phone. Nonetheless, I only had to remind him four times that we were wheels up the following Monday. I wonder what goes through the mind of someone when you ask for this big a favor? Maybe I don't want to know. This is truly the mark of a good friend.

The first day wasn't too bad, but as dusk approached, my truck began losing power and could barely make 50 mph. This 1952 junker that Henry Ford must have worked on personally, had nine billion miles on the odometer and was leaking fuel and spraying it all over the truck behind me...which would be Stan's. Even with the pouring rain and his smeared windshield, I could easily see the question in his eyes, "Why did I agree to do this?" I saw that same look again when we stopped at a greasy spoon for dinner, and later when we got our first glimpse of the rooms at Motel 5. We 'McGyvered' the fuel leak and resumed our trip the next morning, but our undercooked egg choice for breakfast would slow us down more than mechanical problems. We made way too many unscheduled, but entirely necessary, stops at every rest area bathroom south of Memphis. By day's end, we were exhausted and drained, but had finally reached our destination, a storage facility just a mile from the new house. I must not have mentioned to Stan that we'd also be unloading all this furniture into a 10 x 16 garage unit, as I once again saw that 'look' come over his face. It only took two more hours before we would get finished and turn the U-Haul in for a rental car. I found a much better hotel for our last night, and hoped to boost Stan's spirits with massive amounts of alcohol, a great dinner, and the next day's round of golf on a nice course.

On the flight back home I looked across the aisle and nodded to my friend. "Thanks. I'm not sure how I could have done this without you." His response was fun and witty... "I didn't know that was actually an option". Such a kidder. I knew in that moment we'd either be friends for life or he'd never speak to me again. I wonder how he's been.

A Clean Slate

In the process of building your life, you meet thousands of people and, if lucky, eventually put a list together of a dozen or so close friends. These are people you trust and whose opinions you value above all others. This becomes a network of individuals who trade thoughts, dreams, ideas, and often... gardeners, hair dressers, and auto mechanics. Somebody in this group knows at least one person who can fix what you broke, find what you lost, and clean what you got dirty. When you make the decision to retire and move out of state, your friends may still be your closest confidantes, but are of little help when it comes to finding a trusted plumber in a new city. I miss my 'people'.

The first time I needed a haircut here, I thought of Callie who had cut my hair for the past 20 years. Excellent barber...or should I say beautician? (Nah, too 1960's). How 'bout stylist? (Nope...Eighties). So, what do you call a woman who cuts a man's hair these days? Anyway, she knew the right length of the cut and would always squeeze me in between appointments, no matter how busy. I just read the last sentence and need to confirm that Callie has never actually 'squeezed' me. Attention Tim (her husband who once drove a car to Arizona for me): "There was no squeezing prior to our appointments, during, or afterward... uh, what I meant to say was, she would fit me in between other scheduled clients"... oh never mind. Great couple.

I was shaggy on this day and needed a trim, so I begrudgingly stopped at a 'Clip & Curse' in a strip mall near the grocery store. The tiny Asian girl was very pleasant (I think), but not well-versed in the English language. For all I know, she could have been saying, "I'm about to make you look ridiculous and you're going to pay me to do it, and then leave me a big tip, you moron." Assuming that was the translation, she would have been correct. My wife still books a flight home every three weeks when she needs a cut and color. She insists that clause is in her pre-nup agreement. We have a pre-nup?

I am thankful my homeowners association provides a warranty for any maintenance issues we may have with the house. They've been good about fixing the few problems that have arisen. Again, I wouldn't know who to call. Even the landscaping maintenance is covered, which is nice. But the big issue here has been finding the right person for house cleaning. Who doesn't like a clean house? And my wife insists on it. She encourages (threatens) me to help her 'pick up' on a daily basis, and is one of those people who vacuums before the cleaning lady arrives, so as to keep up appearances. Of course, dusting and wiping are part of the pre-maid routine. And you can't have any dirty laundry in the hamper. Oh and the dishwasher must be run and emptied the night before. Back in Iowa, we had the absolute best maid... or should I say domestic? Don't start that again. 'Marsha' knew just the right amount of Pine-Sol to put in a bucket, and was always one step ahead of the 'white-glove test'. She was great. My wife wanted her to move to Florida with us, but her teenage kids might have been a little much. Thankfully, there are these silly rules of an age-restricted community, or I'd be driving her three monsters to school every morning.

For our first domestic helper we took the advice of our next door neighbor, who hails from New Jersey. I only mention that because she offered her maid's services and then said, "If she doesn't do a good job for you, I will send her back to Guatemala and have her family wacked." We all laughed, but I got an eerie sense about 'Ms. Joisy'. I think she said her husband was a Don? My wife admitted her own high standards and explained that the last four temps did not meet our expectations. What expectations do I have? If I do all the actual house chores before she arrives, how tough is it to clean a couple of toilets? As I was heading out the door to play golf, I could tell this new temp was coming today... the house looked pretty darn good.

When I returned later and set my golf bag inside the front door, I knew there was hope. The house smelled terrific and everything was gleaming. There was a note on the counter from the new gal and twenty bucks. "Your wife left me the check for the amount we agreed on. But the house was already so clean, I decided to wash the windows and clean out the closets. I cannot in good faith take so much money, so I am returning twenty dollars. I also noticed your big screen only gets basic cable, so I had my cousin stop by and add the movie channel and sports package to your line-up. He fed an upgrade line off your neighbor's house. I hope that is okay. Buffalo wings are in the oven. See you next week."

Oh my... I think we've hit the jackpot with this one. I stuffed the bill in my shirt and tore up her note. I better get at those wings and clean up the evidence before my wife gets home. I'll be looking forward to an extra twenty with wings every Wednesday.

Critters

No matter which state you reside in, there are cohabitants you certainly could get along without. There are rattlers in the mountains, scorpions in the desert, and meddling in-laws in the plains. Every zone has its challenges. Back in the Midwest, our biggest fear was the occasional skunk or coyote coming out of the woods. But the coyote is afraid of humans and the skunk is afraid of, well nothing... except maybe his stripe turning like Jay Leno's hair as he gets older. And now that we've moved to Florida, there are new critters for us to watch out for. Retirees take heed.

I first encountered fire ants on a previous trip here to play golf. My friend from Orlando, we'll call him Bob (because that is his name), was moving his Titleist away from a small, sandy mound just off the fairway. He took the free drop, announced "ant hill", and proceeded to play the hole. From where I sat, he should have taken an unplayable lie, one penalty stroke, and scored a bogey not a par. I would have contested it, were it not for a few holes later when I hit a 7-iron out of a similar mound of dirt. Splashing 300 tiny red ants all over you would seem harmless, but they didn't stop biting until their itty-bitty ant jaws became tired. My face and arms looked like I had the measles, and my skin was on fire...thus the name.

I can't tell you much about snakes. I've never been a big fan of their darting and slithering, and quite frankly, even a common-variety Garter freaks me out. So you can imagine my horror when I found out the harmless King snake's stripes (red, black, and yellow) look very much like those of the deadly Coral snake, both indigenous to Florida. The locals distinguish between the two by saying, "Red next to black, safe for Jack--red next to yellow, kills a fellow." Really? To be safe, I avoid anything in those three colors and stay away from all men named Jack.

Gators are everywhere. They love fresh-water ponds, and Florida is one big pond with splotches of land scattered about so Wal-Mart has someplace to put up their stores. But the gators like Wal-Mart, too. I saw a 7-footer in the parking lot there this morning; probably looking for a handbag to match her belt and shoes. The natives (that would be anyone from the Northeast that's been here 2 years or longer), hardly notice these imposing reptiles. It is an everyday sighting for anyone playing golf, and if you live near water (stupid statement), you will encounter one regularly. They are surprisingly quick for their size and short legs. How fast do you have to run to escape the clutch of their massive jaws? Just faster than at least one other member of your foursome. That may be an old joke, but I've been doing daily wind-sprints to the mailbox since hearing it.

A newt, a lizard, and a gecko all walk into a bar. OK, surely there's a joke there. I wouldn't know one from the other (although they probably do), but one of them is waiting outside every doorway in Florida. They greet you the second you come up the walk, kind of like insurance salesmen. Is GEICO's headquarters here? That gecko looks familiar. They are startling but harmless, and eventually you'll come to love them. They eat bugs and Florida definitely has their fair share of those.

I have learned so much about nature here in just a few short weeks: a) a ball lying near a gator is a free drop, b) a ball nestled in an ant hill is a free drop, c) if you see a snake, get in your cart and move on to the next hole (your score is par), and finally, d) a ball within five feet of anybody's front door is probably out-of-bounds, and even the locals haven't figured out how to get a free drop from a gecko ...yet.

Weather the Storms

The Florida Chambers of Commerce are very good at their jobs. Websites boast art and culture, museums, sun-drenched white sand beaches, and orange sunsets. I see boats and golfers and tropical landscapes, and my mind is held hostage by dreams of living in this paradise. There is no fine print at the bottom of the page, but if there were it would read: "In every life, a little rain must fall." A little rain? It is currently raining so hard there are buckets filled with cats and dogs coming down. I just checked the garage to see if I had enough lumber to build an ark. These marketing wizards are no slouches. They omitted the fact that it rains in the Sunshine State every day at 4:30 pm. And if by some chance it doesn't rain that day, it will rain for the next three days in a row. I didn't read one article about hurricanes, but in our two months as residents, we've endured "Dennis" and "Wilma" in the central part of the state. The east and west coasts have entertained all the other letters of the alphabet between 'd' and 'w', and there's more on the way. Back in the Midwest, we got nervous with 3 inches of rain. We've had nine inches this morning alone. How great is this paradise thing.

There is nothing to do here when it rains this much. No golf, horse racing, or jai-alai (whatever that is). And the movie theaters are jam-packed. We have yet to resort to board games, but I've been studying the dictionary in case my wife surprises me with a Scrabble challenge. I can't tell you how happy I am we moved here. No seriously, I can't tell you. The power is still on, although it is early yet and a lightening strike should fry a hard-drive any minute now. With nothing better to do, I Google Spanish explorers Juan Ponce de Leon and Pedro Menendez de Aviles. They first explored the Florida area and eventually settled St. Augustine in 1565. The rain likely pummeled these poor slobs too, and their report back to the Motherland was something like... "A land of some rain and some shine". I believe a mix-up in translation eventually gave us the 'Some-shine State', etc. I have not seen any sun since last Tuesday. This is depressing.

The boom that shook the house first started with a whip-like cracking noise. This was followed by a deeper bellowing sound, and finished off with a heavy thump. The entire drama lasted only a few seconds, but plenty of time for me to accumulate moisture in my new Nike boxer-briefs. It was not like you could actually see the bolt of lightning that hit, but more that the surrounding atmosphere was engulfed in a hazy blue hue. I had no idea how close to the house this mortar hit until I went outside the next day and found the 18-inch hole in the retaining wall by our fountain. The 40-pound stones were blackened and scattered across my yard near my neighbor's fence. He came out to see if we survived last night's shelling. "You know you moved to Florida's second highest elevation, right? We get thousands of lightning strikes an hour during storms. Exciting, huh?" Thanks for the info, Ron. I have since attached my lightning rod to the shed where he keeps his golf cart. Now the next storm will be truly exciting!

I still have ringing in my ears, and I know it's not the phone. That was toasted by the million-volt blast. The lamp in the dining room hums now, and every time I turn on the garbage disposal, the garage door goes up. I may have to call an electrician. There's a post-apocalyptic feel to all this, but I think the worst is over. Thankfully, my 52" SONY is still working just fine. The high-definition colors are spectacular, like the greens, and the reds and yellows that are...flashing. Is that on the Weather Channel, honey? No, no, not again today. I'm writing those Chamber people.

What's a Lanai?

Growing up in a small town outside of Louisville, I remember meeting Colonel Harlan Sanders of Kentucky Fried Chicken fame. He and his wife Claudia owned a farm in nearby Shelbyville and he was always seen in public sporting his trademark white suit with bolo tie. My aunt told me he could often be seen in a rocker on his veranda, which stretched all the way around the two-story mansion. I had no idea what a veranda was, and she explained it like this: "When you're at the front door of someone's house and they offer you lemonade, you are on their porch. If they offer you a mint julep, you are on their veranda." The older you get, the more words you learn. Vernacularly speaking, the greater your vocabulary, the more omnipresent are you're opportunities to exhibit your mastery of the English language (I think I just hurt my tongue). But that requires the need to remember a bunch of fancy words which, if used incorrectly, can make you sound as sharp as a four-year old. A porch is a porch.

The first time I heard the word 'lanai', I was watching the sitcom Golden Girls and Betty White said she had recently been on the lanai. I thought she was referring to the island in Hawaii, and I missed the punch line. Found in tropical climates, this open-sided veranda is a roofed, outdoor extension of your living space. Opened up through French doors or sliders that can be closed off to keep out unwanted critters and the occasional hurricane, a lanai is usually a well-furnished patio. So it's a porch. And if this decorated outdoor space is completely enclosed by screen fabric, Floridians call it a 'bird cage'. You'll see these on the backs of homes when playing golf and the resemblance to Parakeet Pete's aviary is remarkable. Most often, a pool is inside this cage and the screen works to keep out the mosquitoes, which have their own air-traffic control system here. You do not want to be out at night in Florida, near any body of water, without bug protection... and quinine pills. Consider yourself warned.

Florida does have its share of insects. If you factor in the moisture needed to keep all the tropical plants healthy, the heat and constant humidity, and temperatures that rarely dip below freezing, why wouldn't bugs be happy here? I wonder if our Midwest insects hop on a dog and head south with their snowbird humans. Or maybe they hitch a ride on 'Air Canadian Goose' and travel non-stop to warmer climates. If our bugs stayed in the cold and snow, wouldn't they all just die? Yet sure enough, they always return in the spring with a vengeance. So they must fly south for the winter or risk extinction, right? I tried for years to use this analogy with my wife in hopes of us moving to the south. Hard as it was, I remained alive and healthy through each and every winter cycle and could never prove my theory. Now that we're here full time, I have fond memories of the white, fluffy snow...and wind chills... and shoveling...check that. Temporary insanity. I'm back with you now. I will gladly put up with the 4000 varieties of insects, knowing I will never again have to endure the torture of another Midwest winter. Even the palmetto bugs.

Leave it to the fine and proper folks of the Sunshine State to come up with their own moniker for one of the most common pests in the world. A cute sounding name for what otherwise is, one of nature's unmentionables. Also known as the water bug, these creepy-crawly nuisances with a hard shell can sometimes grow as big as two inches in length. People here have reportedly seen them fly. Yes, it is the American cockroach. And I just saw a palmetto dart across my lanai. Don't you just love the romantic sounds of this tropical paradise?

A Deal Is a Deal

Nobody tells you about 'the deal' when you first arrive. It's a closely guarded secret all the local golfers know, but are unwilling to share with newcomers. It's like a hot stock tip... if everybody jumps on board, somebody will take away the windfall. With so many visitors coming to Florida every year, I understand their reasoning. Don't ruin it for those who play here all year round. Poor babies. The deal is half-price greens fees with a valid Florida driver's license. This unwritten rule is honored at most all courses, but you'll never hear a word spoken about it. These courses rely heavily on non-resident play to pay the bills, and vacationing golfers have a lot of money to unload during peak times. Why is it that people on vacation spend every dime they bring with them? It's as if the money was earmarked as discretionary funds, and to take it back home with them would be improper. I have a senator like that. Explains why t-shirts with stupid sayings on them is a three-billion-dollar a year industry here. The Sunshine State is home to thousands of golf courses and the competition among them is fierce, especially with the status of our current economy. So while golf rates may be the highest during the winter months when more vacationers are here, the courses have to resort to drastic price-cuts for the discerning locals in the off-season to garner a competitive edge. This half-price bonanza likely started as one of those incentive-to-play bargains, but since nobody can actually speak about it, the deal continues on all year, even during high times. The courses don't want to advertise it and make the out-of-towners angry, and the residents are keeping their proverbial traps shut.

The discount procedure is all very covert and hush-hush. At check-in, the gentleman behind the counter is not going to ask you if you are a card-carrying resident. Why would he? He will gladly take the full amount of the fee and act as if nothing is different. But those in the know, take out their wallet, inconspicuously lift their license out of its holder, and slide it gently across the counter in view of the clerk. There is a quick glance, a slight nod, and the price has automatically been reduced by 50%. A tip of the visor and we're headed to the first tee! The entire process takes only seconds, it's incredible.

Getting a drivers license is an entirely different story, however. It's as if the Department of Motor Vehicles knows all golfers are about to get a laminated 'gold card', and they make you pay your dues by standing in line for hours on-end. I was surprised that the nearest license bureau was a 35-minute drive down a narrow little blacktop. Apparently the state doesn't want novice drivers to run into anything while taking the test, so the only things in danger out here are a few scrawny old cows...no, the ones in the field. The non-descript structure was made of concrete block and had a metal roof. It looked like a garage, not a government building. Maybe I could get my oil changed while I wait? There was no air conditioning and just a handful of chairs. And after spending the better part of my morning in line, I found out another secret the locals don't want to share with outsiders.

The first line takes you to a desk where the car czars determine your eventual driving status. Do you wear glasses? Are you a US citizen? Ever been convicted of stabbing a DMV worker after waiting in a 4-hour line? You know, questions like that. After giving them your vitals, you stand against the wall and wait for someone to call your name to get into the second line. It's like triage in emergency care, except they don't care and there's no emergency. I began to notice more and more people getting their name called without standing in the first line. How could that be? When I reached the last desk, I asked. "Well darling, those are the people who called ahead this morning". What? They reserved a spot and got a bye in the first round? Wouldn't you know it; the State of Florida is not going to be outdone by the good folks at Red Lobster when it comes to call-ahead service. Something smells fishy, Wanda. Why am I here again?

Where Are You From?

My wife and I went shopping at Kohl's last week to stock up on some winter items. We had given every stitch of our warm clothes to charity before leaving Iowa, sure that the solar rays of the Sunshine State would be ample warmth for our first December in Florida. Oops, mistake. It does get rather cool here. Now, I'm not talking 'cold', because it never (almost never) freezes here and there is virtually no frost line in the soil. The air temperatures dip below 32 degrees briefly, and while devastating to a grove of oranges, your engine block is not going to seize up. It's all relative. We hail from the Midwest. When we dip, we dive... and spring must arrive before we can pry the tongue off the old flag pole. But long-time residents here have developed some pretty thin blood lines, and when temperatures get down below 60, they break out the hooded parkas and woolen gloves. I sometimes think it has more to do with fashion than warming comfort, though. If they're sporting knee-high boots and furry boas in New York City, you can bet the girls in Miami are wearing the same here (and not just in the gentleman's clubs).

After filling up the cart, we headed to the checkout counter and waited patiently behind a mother of three who was having some trouble keeping her kids all together. With a little assistance from me and my wife, we managed to get the young woman and her baggage to the head of the line. Behind us, a middle-aged woman was fidgeting back and forth, and finally blurted out, "I only have these items and you have an entire cart. You certainly wouldn't mind if this clerk checked me out first, right?" She abruptly edged her way to the front of the line and the cashier glanced at us for our approving nod, which of course we granted. My wife responded, "It would be our pleasure for you to go in front of us, you must surely be in a rush today." The woman did not respond, hastily zipped her plastic through the machine, and bolted out the door without so much as a "thank you" or "kiss my Kohl's card". The clerk apologized and asked, "Are you from the Midwest? I can tell. I moved here from Wisconsin this summer. That rude woman comes in all the time and she is definitely not from the Midwest." We all three had a good laugh and the customers around us smiled.

Mostly, people here don't care where you came from. They do care whether or not you are pleasant or rude; but who you were, or what you did, is usually of little consequence to these folks. Most of them are transplants too, likely retirees seeking the sun and the sand. As long as you don't block the one and kick the other in their face, they are a pretty tolerable bunch. But while disinterested in your origins, it becomes rather obvious to most who hails from where. British accents, southern drawls, and big city impatience are all tell-tale signs of geographical backgrounds. I don't mean to offend (actually that's not true and it's way too late to change my ways), but try as we may to be a melting-pot society, sometimes the peculiar differences in speech and behavior are too much to ignore. Like my granddaddy once said of the people in Florida, "There are a lot of strange ducks on this pond."

I play in the Men's Golf Club three days a week and I am often shocked and amazed at the thoughts and actions of a few of my golfing partners. One is a club-throwing anti-Semite from Oklahoma. Another is a racist from Alabama. Still another is a kleptomaniac from New Jersey (I lose a pair of sunglasses every time we share a golf cart). And there is even an Ohio State fan... how disturbing is that? With representatives from just about every ethnic, racial, and geographic arena knocking heads every week, I'm not sure how we've avoided a second civil war. I told my wife that the banter from these boys is getting brutal, and the congeniality of my Midwestern good manners is starting to wear thin. I may just have to find another group to play with. She made the suggestion to play with a mixed-couples club that does 18 holes and dinner every Sunday. It's only one day a week, but my wife promised to play two other days with me to satisfy my craving, so I agreed. I assumed she was talking golf.

The first Sunday was pleasant and I played pretty well, which always makes for a better experience. The couples were nice and little was discussed about our personal history or background. All in all, my wife and I had a good time and were looking forward to the next Sunday. Each week paired us with new partners, and 'Bob' and 'Alice' were up next. On the tee box of hole #17, Bob asked me if we had played yet with 'Ted' and 'Carol', and if we found them to be an attractive couple? He went on to describe their "incredible hot tub that seats twelve". He suggested we skip dinner on this night and join a few of the couples at their house for cocktails. "Bring a bathing suit if you must", he laughed. I may have been born at night... but it was not last night. And this old bull knows a cow-pile when he sees one. When the final putt dropped on 18, I shoved my wife into our cart and bolted for the clubhouse. I explained on the way home that these people weren't just 'swinging' 7-irons, and we might want to reconsider golf on Sundays.

I may just have to call up that Ohio State fan to see what time the boys are teeing off tomorrow.

You're Never That Old

When we teed off that morning, it was a crisp 52 degrees. This is the temperature at which Floridians bundle up with heavy coats and parkas, and play golf with gloves on. The Men's Club at our course tees it up promptly at 7:30 am, three days a week. Short of a hurricane in the area, we always play. If it's raining, just put on more layers. If there's lightning, tee off with your one iron (thank you Mr. Trevino, you are a funny man). If there is snow, you took the North exit on the Turnpike and need to see your doctor about the early signs of Alzheimer.

The only thing bundled up more than the Florida golfer in the winter months, is their golf cart. Most members here trick their buggy out with the fanciest of amenities. Chrome wheels, special paint jobs, and the weather cover are mandatory. Some get a little carried away with their accessories, and are only limited by their imaginations and bank accounts. The covers are made of heavy plastic and are leather-trimmed. Most are attached with metal snaps and have vertical zippers that serve as doors. When fully battened down, you could ride out a Category 3 in these babies. The dashboard heater seems a bit extreme to me, but I will reserve my critique until I am a resident here longer. I always wear a short sleeve shirt and everyone teases me about being new. I drive a 'convertible' golf cart; no cover, no heater, and no frills.

I left my naked cart near the first tee and climbed aboard with 'Oscar'. He's a great guy from the Northeast who just turned eighty-one last week, and is always bragging about his Polish heritage. His golf cart is a replica of the 1957 Chevy complete with tailfins, whitewall tires, and chrome baby-moon hubcaps. It sits a little higher off the ground and is easier to get in and out of than most carts. There is an actual hinged door instead of zippers and I remember him commenting on the $12,000 price tag. My full-size Jeep isn't worth that and it's got four seats and 200-horses under the hood. We were teamed up against the club champion and his 4-handicap neighbor, so our chance of winning the game that day would be slim. We discussed a strategy, but came to the conclusion that putting the '57 in reverse and backing over them, would be considered poor sportsmanship. Instead we joked and laughed all day and played really poor golf. At the turn, Oscar said, "It's OK. I've been further behind than this and lost."

Somewhere on the back nine, I asked about his 4-score years on this earth and remarked about his 15-handicap and ability to get around so well. He told me that golf and whiskey and women were the keys to a long life. I asked about the woman I saw him having dinner with the other night. "Her name is Delilah, a little young for me, but an absolute sweetheart", he said. "She has been such a comfort since my wife has gone." I told him I thought it was so great that a man of his age could find someone to fill the void after his wife's passing. He said, "My wife didn't die. She ran off with a younger man; he was in his seventies." I quickly changed the subject.

As we headed up the 18th fairway, I asked 'Oscar' if he would be staying for lunch or a beer after the round. The group usually pushed some tables together in the lounge and split up the cash to the winners. "No, not today", he said. "I've got a date." I asked him to say hello to Delilah and he corrected me. "Today I'm going over to see 'Martha' who lives next door to her. It makes Delilah insanely jealous when I pull up in my golf cart and honk the horn. Then tonight, I have a date with Delilah and she will make every effort to win me back. She can be very, very persuasive." Oh, my.

Get to Work

I've seen this before, but never understood the logic behind it. The whole point to retirement is to stop working, right? My wife and I recently played golf with a couple who had both worked at the same company for 38 years, retired at 62 to Florida, and were seemingly enjoying the leisurely life of daily golf. About half way through the round, they announced to us they were about to sell their home and go back to Michigan to open up a Bed & Breakfast. What? The last I checked, the Upper Peninsula still had ridiculous amounts of snow on the ground and wind chills of minus thirty. I didn't want to sleet on their parade, but was dying to ask why anyone would work all those years to amass a retirement portfolio, then dump it into a 1920's Victorian-style mansion, just to bake a few blueberry muffins for perfect strangers?

If this couple were looking to fulfill a passion, a life-long dream, then I get it. But otherwise, why not just volunteer at a soup kitchen? They need your muffin-baking skills, and in the mornings you can talk to the homeless who just slept outside. You won't even have to clean their room. Take some of that cash you are so willing to part with, and make a donation. Don't buy a 90-year old, 14-bedroom house unless you just hate the feel of folding money. Hey, it is not my place to judge.

This couple seemed so determined. Far be it from me to squash their dream. Two years of scrubbing someone else's shower scum will do it for them. My wife gave me that 'raised eyebrow' thing. Do they get training for that as young girls?

This scenario brought to mind another couple we use to hang out with. After years of working for the federal government, they thought it was a great idea to open a bistro. The joke goes something like... "The best way to make a small fortune in the restaurant business? Start with a big fortune." They made it about 10 months before they lost their linguini. Do people leave the workforce one day, and then put their brains on a Greyhound the next? I don't get it; boredom maybe.

I can't imagine going back to work. While I'm beginning to see some of the drawbacks to Florida, I don't know what would make me jump ship and run back home. The humidity here is oppressive when mixed with the heat. There are too many storms, and by the way folks, hurricanes are serious business. The mosquitoes prevent us from sitting outside, but I'd rather look onto our beautiful patio than put up a birdcage. I don't mind the gators I see on the golf course, 'cause I know where they hang out and I stay away from them. But what if I'm disoriented by a hurricane or a swarm of killer mosquitoes, and I stumble into a swamp... then the alligators become a problem, don't they? I need to think of something else.

Guinness comes to mind (my Great Pyrenees Mountain dog... not the Irish stout). Her one passion has always been to chase the UPS truck as it makes its daily delivery to the neighbor's Amway business next door. Now out of shape, and suffering with arthritic hips, she's no longer able to catch the truck as it speeds away, but still lives for that moment when the diesel engine begins its roar to take off. It makes little sense for her to endure the pain in her joints after the fruitless chase is over, but I would never discourage the thrill of the hunt for her. "Go chase 'em gal. Give it your best shot!"

Likewise, my advice to the Michigan couple should be the same. Follow your heart. And I should follow mine... to the nearest bar.   All this talk of shots and chasers; I believe I'll celebrate the opening of their new B & B, with a shot of B&B and a stout chaser. I mean Guinness, not Guinness.

It'll Be a Blue Cross Christmas

I looked up a college friend when we first arrived in Florida, a chiropractor whose office was only a short drive from our new house. I was hoping to find a good barber and mechanic (maybe not one in the same), and the scoop on the best restaurants in town. I knew he'd also be able to recommend other professionals as well, and we could use a doctor and a dentist since we weren't getting any younger. He warned that the closest medical clinic had a bad reputation, and the longer drive to the county hospital would be the better choice. We discovered that truth in only our second month here.

I had no idea what the symptoms of vertigo were, until my wife came down with it a month before Christmas. The constant spinning of the room seemed a horrible experience for her, so I raced her to the hospital in record time. Bobbing and weaving through the bumper-to-bumper traffic on Highway 50, I was able to replicate that dizzy sensation for myself and several other unsuspecting drivers on the way there. And just to confirm, I was not the cause of the accident that put those three cars in the ditch. I was telling the nurse about this 'busy ditch' story, forewarning her of possible injured patients that may show up as a result of that crash. At the same time I was also explaining my wife's symptoms to her, and I think she may have mixed the two stories up. For the record, I did not call my wife a 'dizzy b*tch'. The nurse scowled at me for the remainder of the visit. Medication was prescribed for my wife and she would be fine. But the next time we need medical attention, I may want to give that clinic a try... and skip the hospital (and this nurse).

A week later I was playing golf and hit a tree root on my approach shot to the 15th green. My wrist absorbed all the shock and I was certain I had broken it. After completing the last few holes nearly one-handed, I finally told my wife about the injury and we tried the nearby 24-hour clinic. I now know why they call it that. It took about that long before a doctor would see me and order the X-rays. A possible hair line fracture was evident, but the 23-year old idiot (I mean intern) thought it was from a former injury, and recommended a brace instead of a cast. Bad call, Doc. It still hurts to this day whenever it rains, and here... that's every afternoon at 4:30. I try to use this story to get a few strokes out of my golfing buddies, but they just blame me for going to that clinic in the first place. Where's the sympathy?

In preparation for our first overnight guests, I installed ceramic tile on the lanai so we could all enjoy our screened-in porch for the holidays. I had been moving around big stacks of these heavy tiles all morning. After grabbing one of the fifty-pound bags of mortar, my wife saw me stop abruptly to catch my breath. Wives go into 'Florence Nightingale' mode whenever you bend over and put your hand to your chest. Okay yes, I was having some chest pains, but it did not feel like a heart attack. I have never had a heart attack, but I've seen enough medical shows on TV to know it was likely just strained intercostal muscles. Didn't matter, we were in the car and on the road once again to the county hospital before I could say "angina". It was a false alarm, but the doctor complimented my wife on her quick reaction. Please do not encourage her. And the nurse (same one from last week) just stared at me in disgust the whole time. Seriously, I was not mean to my wife.

When the headache first started, I figured a nap would take care of it. I had not planned on the 2-day siesta that followed, or the persistent high fever and night sweats. My wife had flown back to the Midwest for a board meeting and was unaware of how sick I had become. I noticed a red spot on my leg a few days earlier, but chalked it up to a spider bite maybe. I didn't give it another thought until the swelling turned into a big bruise and I had to go back to the emergency room. This is the fourth medical issue in as many weeks. Is this what retirement is going to be like? And doesn't that nurse ever take a day off? On the way out, her eyes were glued to me and she was mumbling under her breath. I heard that! I am not a 'meanie'... or a 'hypochondriac'. I hope she's up for retirement soon.

Neighbors

I have found over the years, there are many reasons why people move to different locations. Job changes can make you pull up stakes. College and marriage put folks in new places. And now in retirement, we see many of our friends moving away to be closer to their kids and grandchildren. But sometimes, moving is just about escape. For the record, our move to Florida had more to do with winter weather than any other factor. So don't let my 'neighbor-bashing' be seen as the reason for our trek south. The average American homeowner will buy approximately 3.7 houses in his/her lifetime, and we are right on target with that statistic. Our first house was the size of a walk-in closet. We got the 0.7 out of the way early. We built three more after that. That's a lot of neighbors (with a lot of issues), and often times in too close proximity for those of us diagnosed with claustrophobia. I need space.

My wife and I have been blessed with many great neighbors. But honestly, a few were challenging beyond the point of exhaustion. I remember a young Wisconsin man in our first neighborhood, whose wife had just left him. He would sob his way across the street every weekend and end up at our kitchen table looking for sympathy. Try as I could, I lacked the compassion of my wife. She listened intently and consoled his breaking heart. One Friday, she was out of town when 'Dork' (I'm pretty sure that was his name) came over drunk and professed to me, his undying love for my wife. He vowed to "steal her heart and run off with her", and was serving me notice that all is fair in love and war. I tossed the little cheese head out on his ear and explained that there would likely be a lot more war than love, in his near future. My wife may have been startled by the 'FOR SALE' sign in our front yard when she returned, but never said much about it.

Our next home was a new, custom-built, two-story 'Street of Dreams' beauty, complete with every possible upgrade. "Sign here, pick out your carpet, and move in tomorrow." How easy is that? It was a very kidsy community and, while we didn't have children of our own, everyone seemed friendly and made us feel welcome. The next door neighbor had four kids, all with red hair, all under the age of five. Collectively, their screaming could reach the decibel level of an F-16 taking off... in my bathroom. And the cute little tykes liked to take turns unlatching the gate to let our dogs out of the fenced-in yard. While my wife, when mad, may sometimes accuse me of behaving like a 2-year-old, I could not find a way to reason with these little monsters. Escape was our only hope. To this day, I don't know how those kids got locked in that garden shed out back. Freak accident, I suppose. Shortly after that, we started looking for multiple acres on the outskirts of town. I need more space, apparently.

It took the realtor a few months to meet the criteria for our next house. Our wish list included a pond on ten acres, a babbling brook (isn't that just a stream that talks too much?), with horse farms and cornfields for neighbors. She found it and we escaped to a rural paradise. Lots of space, thank you.

We enjoyed the squirrels, the geese, and an occasional coyote... as long as he wasn't feasting on the squirrel or the goose. And though the Iowa winters were always a challenge on that property, we were thankful to be such an integral part of Mother Nature's domain. To get a break from the snow, we took trips every year to Arizona and fell in love with the mountains, the never-ending sunshine, and the dry February weather. There was no doubt our future would someday include a home where we could play golf year round, wielding a seven-iron instead of a snow shovel.

Now that we've retired and settled here in central Florida, I can't find anything wrong with the folks that live on this block. The houses may be a little close together 'cause I can read the clothing tags on my neighbor's underwear without binoculars. Hey, if she didn't want me to look, she would close the blinds. They all seem nice, standing out in their yards, when I drive by. I see them wave and I wave back, and soon I will actually go meet them... someday. There's no rush, we've only been here for five months, and I'm currently enjoying my space.

Golf Is Fun, Seriously

The plane didn't touch down in Orlando until almost 9:30 pm. My wife and I had flown back home from a funeral and didn't have many options for the weekend return. My folks were visiting us from Kentucky and agreed to stay at the house with our dogs for the few days we would be gone. It was our hope to get back earlier because my dad had made a seven o'clock tee time the next morning on a golf course recommended by one of his friends. Who plays golf at 7 am? With nobody in front of you, a foursome could be finished by 10:00. What on earth are we going to do for the rest of a Saturday...with my parents? Breakfast, immediately followed by lunch, and hopefully a nap. Cocktail hour may need to start a little sooner than normal.

My father has always been an avid golfer, albeit a hack who struggled to break a hundred most of his life. Nothing wrong with hacks, we enjoy the game as much as the next guy. It's a game. It should be fun. He always joked that he had shot his age many times, and unlike the pros, only needed fifteen holes to accomplish the feat. He taught me the game when I was ten years old, and now with him in his seventh decade, I'm just happy we're playing together today. It's weird that we're both retired now. I seldom got the chance to play golf with him when we were both working. We lived in different states and I was not good about visiting. My mother never took up the game and I always thought that was such a shame, until today (I will come back to this). The experiences my wife and I have shared on so many golf courses, from Hawaii to Ireland, have given our marriage many great memories. Today would not be one of them.

It was pitch-dark as we were getting our clubs out of the car and lacing up our soft spikes. None of us had played this course before, and I was anxious to see the track. My wife had just come off a round of 85 on our home course, and was chomping at the bit to get back out for 18 more. Mother was the fourth for our group, somehow talking my father into tagging along for the round. She promised to ride quietly in the cart and insisted this outing would bring us all closer together as a family. How do you argue with that? It was my understanding she had never set foot on a golf course before this day, taking no prior interest in my father's scores, experiences, or the rules of the game. These fears were confirmed with her first questions. "Are you really going to take all those clubs out there today? Why not just take the ones you need? If you each took three or four, you could share. It doesn't seem like a friendly game if you're not allowed to share. If you ask me, it makes more work for everybody involved." We hadn't asked.

The starter announced our name and starting time, "You're up! Tee off now or lose your spot!" It was still dark. I could not see the fairway, or the green, or the flag. It seemed silly to launch a perfectly good Titleist into the abyss with no chance to recover it. And then I quickly realized I do that on most of my tee shots, and daylight seldom makes much difference. So, off we go. None of us found our first shots on this par-3, but nearly stumbled into the pond to the left of the green. Were you aware that an alligator makes a deep snorting sound when mating, and possibly when retrieving a five-dollar, Pro V1 golf ball? The sound was loud and seemed close by and I did not search very long or very hard. I suggested we each take the score of par for our blinded efforts and move on to the 2nd hole. My mother immediately took issue with this, and just before she spit out the word "cheating", my dad turned around and gave her 'the look'. I may have been apart from my parents for many years, but I remember that look. It would stop a charging moose in its tracks. Mother Moose walked quickly back to the cart and took her seat. We all need to focus on the fun of this game.

My mother spent most of the remaining front nine asking my father questions about the rules of the game, and I was thankful she was sharing his cart and not mine. As we continued onto the back side, her opinions became more vocal again. On the thirteenth hole she questioned why anyone would wash their golf ball and then hit it into the pond. I tried to ignore her and refused to engage her outrageous comments. I was having enough issues with my faltering game, and my wife was struggling as well. My dad had gone through a dozen golf balls already and might have shot his age about three holes back. We all three landed our approach shots onto the seventeenth green but missed our putts. Mom turned to dad and said, "Why didn't you putt that last one into the hole? You were so close and it was the same distance as the one before it. What happened? It doesn't appear to be that tough of a game. No wonder you're never happy with your score when you come home."

I didn't think we'd see 'the look' twice in the same day. Actually this was a day of many firsts for me. I had never left a golf course after seventeen holes, even if it was pouring down rain. I had never teed off in complete darkness before today. Taking my mother along as a spectator would be a first... and a last. And witnessing my father throw a club into the pond completed a full day. I will have to buy him a new putter for our final round tomorrow, before they head back home to Kentucky. My mother chimed in, "Maybe you could just share?" I'm not sure what she will be doing on her last day here.

Vanity

This is a word that got me in trouble today, and I'm quite sure it's not what you think. My wife and I have a plumbing problem, no not the renal kind...an actual leaky pipe in the master bath. This is a brand new house and there is hot water coming out from under my wife's sink cabinet. Apparently it is called a 'vanity' because of the mirrors, a series of gigantic reflecting panels that resemble the Hubble Space Telescope. You

can honestly see the entire Eastern seaboard by looking into the glass on her side of the bathroom. There is what I like to call, the 'big screen', a 6' x 8' piece of glass that covers the entire west wall. This is flanked by two full-length mirrors, one on the left and one on the right. At just the correct angle, you can watch yourself see the other side of you staring at the backside of your body from the front. Why on earth would anyone want to do that? I tried it naked once and will never be able to erase that picture from my brain. There is also a magnified mirror that swivels and flips 360 degrees. When the early morning sun is focused on the sidewalk across the street, it can set a colony of red ants on fire (a little experiment I tried one day when my wife was at the mall). This is no kids toy. We can pick up radio signals from Cuba on rainy days, and I've never had to pay extra for the NFL TICKET. Whatever it is she needs to see that badly, I want no part of.

But now it's all gone. Not the water, the entire bathroom. They've taken out the vanity with mirrors and the drywall, down to the studs. Workers ripped out the tub and shower and most of the gorgeous tile my wife had picked out. The warranty department determined that a polystyrene pipe was split near the base of the wall, and had probably been leaking since day one. Most of the water had escaped to the outside, which explains why our azalea plant on the left of the house, is twice the size of the one on the right. Because they found one spot of mold on the wall, they sent in an environmental hazmat team to completely rid the area of any debris. It was all a little too 'E.T.' for me, what with these geeks walking around all day in their moon suits. "One small step for my bathroom, one giant leap...". They walled off the bath with a zippered-plastic door, installed an exhaust tube out the window, and hermetically sealed the room. They estimated three to five weeks to replace it all, and I figured the divorce decree would likely take that much time as well. But, my wife said she'd be OK making other arrangements, and I might have been a bit leery. Women say they want to share everything with their spouse; feelings, closeness, bank accounts. But in reality, their space in the bathroom is sacred. "Danger, Will Robinson! Danger!"

And now we come to the heart of my dilemma. I of course, agreed to give her the full use of the guest bathroom for the next month, thinking that gesture will solidify my place in the Husband Hall of Fame. With shaving kit in hand, I proceeded down the hall to the half-bath nearest the foyer. Who takes half a bath? And with only a pedestal sink and a toilet, which water washes which parts? It doesn't sound too sanitary. I may have to splash on a little extra cologne before leaving the house. My wife stopped me dead in my tracks. "You can't use that bathroom. What will our neighbors think if your stuff is in the powder room? They'll think we're having marital problems." Tell the neighbors to pee before coming over. I shuttled past her, closed the door, and shaved my face, wiping my whiskers all over the guest towel. Where do women get these crazy notions? Tell me that was not the doorbell that just rang.

Just a Game, Right?

After my parents went into retirement mode and shuttled off to Florida, my mother would often get out her area map and drag my father along on daily explorations of the territory within 50 miles of their house. Covering that distance in high-season bumper-to-bumper St. Petersburg traffic, could take most of an afternoon. This is the part where I could insert criticism about the stereotypical 'Florida driver', but that is way too easy a target and to be honest, I've seen worse drivers in many other parts of the country. In their defense, I envy the person who is determined and committed to their destination. So much so, that running stop lights and making U-turns without regard to other vehicles, is a sign of perseverance in pursuit of a color, cut, and perm. Who doesn't need to look good for the ladies' euchre tournament luncheon? And if truth be told, when you reach a certain age, you should be entitled to drive as though you own the road. Fifty years of taxes has to be good for one county highway, or at the very least, a city street.

On one excursion, my mother spotted an Indian casino and her life would never be the same again. Ten minutes after walking through those doors, she walked up to a slot machine, fed it a ten dollar bill, and hit a $700 jackpot on the first pull. She cashed in the winning ticket, tracked down my father, and bolted out the front door. They couldn't have been on the premises for more than twenty minutes. Her response? "Where could I get a job at my age that pays $2,000 an hour? This is going to work out great for us." My mother returned to that casino every week for ten years, and probably that same machine, and never repeated her one-and-out winning streak. A sad scenario, but one that's repeated far too often in our culture. We have more seniors living below the poverty level than ever before, and it is draining our communities' resources.

Now, it's none of my business whether you blow your life savings (and kids' inheritance) in a gambling house, but I am obligated to report what I see as an industry that preys on a generation of retired folks that are looking to receive the payback they came to expect after all their years of hard work and penny-pinching. And then only to have half their savings disappear in a swap-for-greed banking implosion. I am getting an eerie sense that now having said that, people are lurking in the shadows, stalking me... probably just a hit-man. When did gambling become gaming? "Playing a game for entertainment", sounds better than "gambling away your hard-earned money". So, 'gambling' is bad and 'gaming' is good? For me personally, the reality of 'beating the odds' usually goes something like this: 2 outs, bottom of the 9th, with my team up by 7 runs... my pitcher walks the next 11 batters to lose by one. I couldn't get a date with Lady Luck if I drove a Porsche and promised to share my feelings with her. I am just not good with games of chance, and based on my golf scores this week, lousy at games of skill as well. My good fortune has instead, always come in the form of remarkable social skills and ruggedly-handsome good looks (I will pause for a moment here, to remind you this is my story and my mirror I am looking into, so you can keep that in mind when reaching your own conclusions). Most people would say my luck came from marrying up. They would insist that it is my wife who is drop-dead gorgeous and socially refined... and that I am along for the ride. I hate it when other people are right. Let's move on.

You can't go into a convenience store or gas station where lottery tickets aren't sold. Casino advertising fills the billboards that line the roadways of this great country. We are bombarded daily on our TVs and radios with promises of life-changing possibilities for just one dollar. At some point, who wouldn't believe that it's time for their ship to come in? For most though, that ship is a small dinghy with a leaky bottom (I will pause for another moment here to suggest that these are two things you do not want as you get older). The moral to this story? If it's too good to be true, then what other criteria is required for you to make a sound decision about your savings? And if you're not interested in passing your wealth along to family members when your time comes, be sure you outlive your money by only one day. If everybody would do that, there might be enough left for us starving artists.

Wish I could stay and chat more, but I've got to run to the store before tonight's six-o'clock drawing.

Maintenance Free

There has to come a point when broken things are finally fixed. I'm not kidding here. We've owned several homes and I realize I get anxious and consider selling whenever I have to re-fix what got broken for the second time... or fourth. I fully understand house maintenance. You cannot live in a house and use its moving parts, and not expect to make repairs from time to time. I get it. But it keeps coming and coming. If you fix it correctly once, that ought to be sufficient. And if you replace it once, that should last you. I am still talking about home repairs and not, say marriages, for instance. Although I will give that more thought. I consider myself somewhat handy and usually know how to fix most problems. Today would not be a testament to that. I am having issues with my low-voltage landscape lights. Yes, I checked the bulbs; and I checked the breakers and the G.F.I. switches. I have power going to the transformer, but it's just not lighting things up. Actually, my wife used those exact words last night in the bedroom... never mind. It has to be a connection to one of the fixtures, but two weeks ago I re-attached the wires to each one of them, so that can't be the problem. I'm tired of the hassle and have reached my frustration threshold. Yesterday, the spa would not heat up. Last week it was the fountain on the patio... again. When will it stop? Does it stop?

I envisioned retirement as a "maintenance-free lifestyle". I read the sales brochure... that's what they promised. My wife and I would enjoy leisurely walks around the lake, daily golf on lush green fairways, and evenings on our patio overlooking the pool... that is beautifully lit up at night when the #$%^&* landscape lights work. I did take my leisurely walk this morning, but it was down the aisles of every hardware store on the planet looking for a matching transformer plug that fits my lighting system. There was golf today on my course, just not by me. And this evening, staring into complete darkness, probably won't be all that pleasant if my wife asks me why the patio lights still aren't working.

I will admit she makes sense; there are legitimate times to call a repairman.   I agree whenever it involves major electrical work, especially after the 'brother-in-law incident.' Okay, so apparently if you hook all the white wires together and all the black wires together in a 3-gang switch and turn the power back on, the thick smoke makes it difficult for a near-sighted, unnamed family member to see the hanging pot rack in the kitchen. He should have known it was there, it's his house. It was only six stitches. And while the charred drywall did require four coats of paint, the smell only took a few days to dissipate. It's not like we had to call the fire department. They only showed up because of the paramedics. I also yield to the trained professionals when major plumbing is required. I can change out drains and toilets, but sweating pressure lines together always looks like I spilled some copper on a lot of solder.

To my credit, I have successfully replaced three dishwashers for neighbors, and not once have they mentioned any water leaks or drain problems. Odd that I haven't actually heard from any of them lately... they must be very busy.

At three o'clock this morning the smoke alarms started beeping. Half asleep, I figured I was either on fire or needed to change some batteries. I vaguely recall the rule where you're suppose to change smoke alarm batteries every time you set your clocks forward... or is it backward? I can never remember, obviously. If you live in a state that doesn't observe Daylight Savings Time, do you and your wife alternate shifts so you don't die in the fire? Why can't they make permanent batteries that you only have to put in once? I looked all over but could not find any of those square 9-volt batteries in the drawers and cabinets. I calmly explained to the alarm fixture that there was no fire, but it kept beeping anyway. I promised it I would visit the hardware store first thing when it opened in the morning. It just ignored me. Beep... beep...beep.

The next day I was able to find a brand new smoke alarm at the same store that sells drywall. Good thing. Who knew a hammer would actually stop that incessant beeping... and make such a big hole in the ceiling? That's it. I'm calling a realtor.

And based on my wife's comment regarding a lack of power in the bedroom, maybe a marriage counselor. If it breaks more than once...

Boomerang

Some people said my wife was homesick. I assure you, that was not the case. She flew back to Iowa every two or three weeks for a board meeting or family function, and didn't miss anything that was going on back there. Others said I was homesick, and we are pretty sure those people have never met me. Family? What family? I flew back once for a friend's funeral, and as much as I miss him... he isn't likely to show up for my wake. For me, Florida represented a destination beyond the stress of a working world, where the bright sun, warm breezes, and rolling tides made the thought of getting older just a little easier to endure. With short drives to Cape Canaveral and Disney World, I would be able to escape this planet and its troubles whenever I wanted. Throw in a daily round of golf and it seemed as though this fantasy lifestyle would allow me to go on forever. My fountain of youth. And after fifty, you start looking a little harder for that fountain. So I figured a state surrounded by water would be the ideal choice, don't you agree? While perfect for some, turns out this just isn't the place for us to dig in for our last stand. It would be difficult for me to pick just one reason for our decision to leave the Sunshine State. There were probably many.

It could have been the house. We built a beautiful home on a bluff overlooking the fairway and a lakeside green. Great sunsets. And while the developer was able to sell all the lots in this community, he ran into some legal trouble with shoddy construction issues on a few of the homes. Lawsuits were filed and the H.O.A. was struggling with some infrastructure problems. Our house was built well, but probably because we rented a house across the street during construction in order to oversee the quality of the work. I had to confront the builder with mistakes almost every day and that left a sour taste in my mouth. It did not help that he was an Ohio State fan. My wife and I felt sorry for the neighbors who had to deal with major structural flaws. But that was not the sole reason for leaving.

There is no question that the Florida weather was a challenge for us. The sun and the warm temps were great, but we timed our arrival to this paradise during its record hurricane season. The twenty-eight storms that battered the coasts and crossed inland over a five-month period, probably never allowed us to get fully settled in. There is a lot of rain in this state. No wonder everything is green and beautiful. So weather is the reason? Here we are seriously considering going back to the snow and cold...like somehow that's better. So let's review... a beautiful home that's not in the snow. What exactly is the problem here? Maybe this whole notion to move back to the Midwest was my wife's idea, so she wouldn't have to fly back and forth as much. She brainwashed me (over the years, my wife has suggested that would not be a difficult feat). Perhaps I was hypnotized. Or what if she slipped me a Mickey... or a Minnie? Yes, that's it, I'm in a trance. Help me!

I would be the first to admit, as nice as they were, we never spent much time with our new neighbors here in Florida. Any time I was not on the golf course (every day), I was running my wife to and from the airport. I think we were well-liked in the community... at least I never came home and found anybody picketing in front of our house. And we went to a few block parties and weren't asked to leave. All-in-all, I'd say the neighborhood was okay... just not really that warm and fuzzy. So, I can't blame our abrupt exit on our neighbors.

They never said anything, but I could tell our dogs did not like Florida. There were no fields to run in, no other dogs their age to play with, and lapping water out of the nearby ponds could be intimidating with an alligator watching you. Maybe that's why there were no other dogs in the neighborhood. And may have self esteem issues, evidenced by their struggles to 'take care of business' with other people looking on. They were not used to an audience. But as long as they're fed on time, get petted often, and are allowed lengthy naps, they can exist just about anywhere. It would be safe to say we didn't leave because of unhappy dogs. Anyway, as a society we tend to blame 'it' on the dog far too often. It would be nice if we could pin our departure on one thing or some body, but I guess we just never let Florida soak in (pun intended with all due respect to the 177 inches of rain last fall). We kept it at bay (no pun) for the short time we were here, and bailed (yes, pun again) before we got a chance to find our way.

We did play some great golf courses though, and that was both good and bad. Lots of fun, but I played really badly most of the time. Still that by itself was not reason enough to pack up and leave. I was playing bad long before moving to Florida.

We visited friends that live in other parts of the state, just not that often. We traveled up and down both coasts to see the sights, but it mostly all looked the same to us. We enjoyed the sunrises and the sunsets, and I wouldn't trade the experience for anything, but I'm pretty sure the sun rises and sets in every other state... not sure about North Dakota. It was almost as if we were on an extended vacation, not like a permanent move. My wife never even got her Florida drivers license. We weren't here long enough to see our names in the phone book. AARP never tried to contact us here. We still have boxes to unpack. Our friends from Leesburg call our brief time here, 'the annulment period'. Nice.

Tough as it was, the decision has been made and we need to start thinking about our return plans. What will people back in Iowa think? I'll tell you what, they'll think we're nuts! At some point we may have to acknowledge that we made a mistake moving to Florida. What, admit that we were wrong? No, that won't do. We tossed the boomerang into the wind (albeit a Category3 named Wilma) and it took us in one direction, but brought us back to square one. There must be a good reason for that. Thankfully, I've got a two-day drive ahead of me... to make up a reason.

Back to Square One

As we were driving north on I-75, I couldn't help but notice the empty billboards. There were banners stretched across them saying, "Call Bill at 123/456-7890 to Rent This Sign". It became quite clear to me at that moment why the signs are referred to as 'Bill' boards. I never knew before. I recall the other sides of these same panels on the way down to Orlando, marking exit after exit, touting "Fun in the Sun" and "Land of the Sand". These ads were so welcoming and promised us a tropical paradise for our new-found retirement. The move to the Sunshine State was so exciting, yet our return trip to the Heartland seemed so anti-climactic. It was sad and a bit eerie as we crossed over the state line into Georgia.

I find it hard to believe we were only there for eleven months, seemed like twelve. We packed a lot in that brief period, including 28 hurricanes and many rounds of bad golf. But Florida was not the place for us, and my wife and I sat quietly in the car as we cruised along the highway back to our old life. Having left earlier than us, our worldly possessions were likely a few hundred miles ahead of us on a moving truck. No rental vans this time around, as I was out of energy and friends to beat up on. "Leave it to the professionals", my wife said. Good call. Our stuff would go into storage until our next house got built.

Our temporary new home is a hotel that offers extended stays. I'm pretty sure that these people have no idea what they are in for. My two dogs are very well behaved but they are used to roaming off the leash. Actually, the same can be said for my wife. The four of us cooped up in this mini-suite for three months will be anything but sweet. I fully expect the company will review their policy regarding length-of-stays, after we have taken up homestead here for a while. And with free breakfasts and free happy hours every day, I just may decide to stay here and lay off my building contractor for say, five years? If this hotel would throw in a dog-walking masseuse, I might just sell my new property outright.

The first couple of weeks in 'Shangri-la' were pretty good. The dogs and I drove out to the property every day to watch the builders work. They liked having acreage in which to run wild and chase squirrels... the dogs, not the builders. My wife spent her days picking out window coverings, paint colors, and those feminine touches that every new house screams for. And our nights, while a little too close for comfort on occasion, were mostly uninteresting... until the new neighbor took up residence next door.

I had seen this gal in the parking lot a few times, but didn't know she lived in the next suite. At first glance when I answered the door, I thought the maid had dropped her fuzzy Venetian blind cleaner outside our room. But then, the tiny dog with fluffy white hair moved suddenly and I called to my wife to toss me the pet spray bottle for 'accidents'. Like I said, it moved rather suddenly and I really had to go anyway. This was no ordinary pooch, and had likely been bred in the designer-sweater section at Macy's. I could not see its beady little eyes, and, yes, I am sure they were beady. The nipping was followed by yipping, and subsequently by darting and zipping. I saw my dogs actually smile before I could slam the door to halt the launch of their attack. I could not have made my dogs happier if I had taken them to PetSmart to pick out any toy on the shelf. It happened so quickly. At last sighting, they were slap-pawing tiny Sabrina like a hockey puck down the hall and through the legs of the ice machine. My wife did not see the humor as I lifted my arms and yelled, "GOOOOOOOOOAL!" Nor did the new neighbor. As my wife was introducing herself... and apologizing... I slipped out the door and down the hall for the day's happy hour. I hope they have those little mini pizza bites again tonight. I may not get dinner.

Buy It, Sell It, Buy It Back

The old adage goes something like this: "If you haven't used it in the past year, get rid of it". I'm pretty sure the author of that phrase was talking about possessions and not people, but I will give that some more thought later. Our move to Florida (and back) has given us the opportunity to amass a large amount of stuff. I have learned during this process for instance, that a couch that works in the decorating scheme of one house, does not necessarily work in another. I don't fully understand the reasoning behind this, but it is supported by every woman in America. An Iowa couch cannot be a Florida couch; regardless of the color and material or that the room is the same size and configuration. I don't get it. Man is from Mars and Woman is from Venus, and therefore it is not possible to explain the thoughts and actions of one as it relates to the other. So the sofa we took to Florida was replaced by a new one, and that one was replaced when we came back... and that's that. Want to buy a couch?

The owner of the storage facility smiles when he sees me drive up to his compound. He has added a new row of garages since we went south, and informed me of his expansion plans and recent purchase of adjacent land. You'd think he would have consulted me first, since he bought it with my money.

I'm happy for him, really.

If it were just the couch, I would not be so perturbed, and so broke. But with every new sofa comes its 'accessories', which are also deemed incompatible when moved from state to state. I am learning so much in retirement. I may have to go back to work in order to pay for all this knowledge. As I loaded the coffee table into the space next to its matching end tables, I noticed that the last set I dropped off here, looked amazingly like the ones we just bought yesterday. When I approached my wife with this discovery, she insisted that those pieces would never work with the new house décor; nor would the nine framed pictures or dozens of pillows. Don't get me started on the candle holders and centerpieces. Want to buy a buffet? (Be warned: It apparently has nothing to do with unlimited trips to the salad bar).

Paying monthly rent to house a virtual furniture store doesn't make good sense. So, my wife was initially okay with the idea of a garage sale. And I pictured the extra cash going toward a new set of golf clubs for the man of the house. Shedding unwanted clothes and furniture would be a great way to declutter our lives, and the challenge of 'letting go' would be a mark of self-discipline. We had already given countless boxes of clothes to charity with the sale of each house, but there were still so many in my wife's closet, that plenty would be available for sale. I had already pared down to six golf shirts, a few pairs of jeans, and three pairs of shoes. This skimpy collection is normal for men in retirement. What else would we wear? Add a blazer, a blue dress shirt, and a pair of khakis, and we're good to the end of time. The above ensemble will work well for a wedding or a funeral, and I have found that my attire has never once bothered the recently deceased. I realize that women have a different take on this wardrobe thing though, so I won't pretend it will be easy for my wife to downsize. But who needs ninety three pairs of shoes? And fourteen pairs of black pants? Do we really expect the washing machine to be down for two weeks? There are four seasons to dress for, so keeping colors in multiples of four might be justifiable. But seriously, some of this stuff could go.

The thought of earning extra cash for these discarded treasures all sounded pretty good until we started 'the list'. The purpose was to catalog all items, sorting those the family might be interested in, from the ones that would go to the sale. This list was handed out at our house during a family birthday party, and soon after, a re-enactment of Black Friday at Walmart broke out. It was not pretty and was over in eleven minutes. The family took everything not bolted down, and I'm worried my wife doesn't have enough clothes left to get to the mall tomorrow without being arrested for indecency. I knew we should have given the church the remainder of her clothes. The composure and dignity that were lost on that day, can never be recovered (side note: consider my sister-in-law as a first-round pick at our Thanksgiving day football game).

I regret that we followed up the next weekend with a family trip to the storage warehouse. Our nieces and nephews wasted no time, and no shame, picking out furniture and accessories for their apartments. Apparently a Florida couch does fit into an Iowa decorating scheme, if you are single and under 25. The concept of 'free' may play a role in that acceptance. Even my wife's siblings exchanged couches and tables for the ones we were going to sell. There was ultimately no garage sale and no new set of clubs for me. I am paying the same monthly rent for storage as before, only now filled with the family's stuff. How is that fair? I did consider myself lucky to be able to snag my old bag of clubs from the garage before the family pilfering, until I lost fifty bucks on the golf course today. Next time I'm going to post everything on eBay. Do they take families?

St. Joseph Is for Real (Estate)

I could not in good faith, accept the five one-hundred dollar bills and pushed them back across the table. The look on my wife's face was surprise... followed by disbelief... followed by whatever look goes with, "You're an idiot". But, I had already promised this treasure to someone else and was going to stick by my word. The treasure in question, is a three-inch plastic statue of St. Joseph and this is his story.

My wife and I had been anxious to sell our Florida house, especially on the front-end of what eventually became the worst housing debacle in U.S. history. It was 2007 and the market was showing signs of stress just as we decided to move back to Iowa. We lived in a gated, golf community that had restrictions on 'FOR SALE' signs in yards, and were only allowed to put a small placard in the front window. Who would see that? So, we let the word out in the neighborhood and hoped to sell it on our own without paying a realtor's commission. In addition, we had heard of a sales gimmick (hocus pocus?) using a small, plastic statue bought from a religious supply store. We purchased this St. Joseph statue, complete with directions on how to bury him in the yard next to the front sidewalk. For six bucks, it seemed a harmless (hopeful) way to have some fun in starting the process. In less than one week, a knock on our door came with a full-price offer, cash, no realtor, and no contingencies. SOLD.

About a month later, I was remodeling a rental property after a tenant had moved out, and decided it was time to get out of the landlord business. Over coffee that morning, my wife and I had just discussed the amount of money we had wrapped up in this rental, and what it would take to sell it, albeit in a very depressed market. I had opened up all the windows and doors that day, and was painting the interior when a gentleman walked in to inquire about my plans for the property. He left a deposit check on the counter. St. Joseph was still sitting in the cup holder of the car we brought back from Florida, and that vehicle was parked up on the sidewalk that day while I was working. SOLD. I'm starting to like this little guy.

I was sharing this story with a friend whose daughter had been trying to sell her home with a realtor for two years. I offered the services of my little new best friend, and popped him in the mail that afternoon. Two weeks after she buried the statue and recited the required prayer, she accepted an offer on the house and sent St. Joseph back to me. SOLD. Could this really be happening?

A couple from Portland had two houses to sell, one in Oregon and another in Arizona. After telling his short story, I offered to send these good friends my 'Plastic Peddler' and they buried him in front of their Phoenix house. Three weeks later... SOLD. 'Gail' dug up St. Joseph (putting a small gash in his tiny acrylic leg), stashed him in her purse, and flew to Portland the next day to check on her other house for sale. While waiting for her realtor and standing on the sidewalk in front of that home, a lady drove up and asked to go through the house. SOLD. Yep, St. Joseph was still in her purse and she hadn't even had time to bury him yet.

My wife and I made plans to go to Phoenix and would meet up with Gail and her husband to celebrate their good fortune and retrieve our statue. They had friends staying with them, one a realtor named 'Jim', and we all went out to dinner that night. Gail had wrapped up my little buddy in white paper, complete with cute little houses on it, and a yellow silk bow. She quietly slid it across the table with a nod and a big smile. Their realtor friend asked about this exchange, and the story was soon unveiled. I explained that it was likely the prayers that sold those houses, and a piece of plastic could not be responsible. But Jim was not hearing any of that. "Five houses, each sold within weeks of burying this St. Joseph?" He thought he had hit the equivalent of a real estate trifecta. It may have been the four empty bottles of wine on the table, or the anxiety and pressure of a depressed real estate market, that caused this otherwise reserved businessman to jump up from his seat and shout, "The Holy Grail!" He couldn't get his wallet out fast enough and slapped the five bills down onto the table. Had it not been for my promise to another friend, I might have parted company with the good saint that day. I mean, come on... it was five hundred bucks!

It would have been wrong for me to sell out to a commercial entity that night, and I believe I did the right thing by turning down the money. My wife brings up the story whenever my sanity is brought into question (more often than I think necessary), and nobody asks me for financial advice after hearing of this incident. Surely luck and coincidence are the only plausible explanations for these miraculous phenomena, but just to err on the side of caution, I've got Little Joe tucked away in my wall safe.

But It's a Dry Heat

I love Arizona in the spring time. The desert flora blooms and the temperature hovers at that comfortable 70 degree mark. The reflection of the sun's rays from South Mountain to the White Tanks, gives the Valley sky that gorgeous blue color only the Southwest knows. And everyday about this time, a breeze will kick up to remind you that you are still earthbound and not yet in heaven. But it is not spring time today, it is July. We thought it would be a good idea to visit Arizona in the summer and experience the heat for ourselves. And not to disappoint, the temperature on my golf cart thermometer just reached 115 degrees and is climbing. There is no breeze today unless you stand close enough when I swing my driver, and that could prove to be fatal the way I'm hitting the golf ball. I have just finished the front nine, but already consumed enough water to fill a camel's hump... and it is only noon. (Side note: This is a desert. Where are all the camels?) Water is a crucial staple in this arid heat. The moisture in your body evaporates quicker than your nest-egg dollars in this bear market. As of late, the only numbers worse than those on my score card are at the bottom of my retirement account statement.

A reporter on the local news actually fried an egg on a downtown Phoenix sidewalk yesterday afternoon. He had two strips of bacon and some toast on a plate next to his demonstration and I would've gladly paid $2.99 for it, gravel and all. Ok, so it's hot. And you always hear, "Sure it's hot in Phoenix, but it's a dry heat". I admit the low humidity keeps the proverbial elephant off your chest when walking to and from your golf cart to the tee box. But it can still burn the paws off a tiger at 120 degrees (elephants, camels, and tigers... oh my... I have this strange urge to visit the zoo). A kitchen oven puts out dry heat too, but would you actually stick your head in there? Or climb inside a dryer? Well not more than once, and that was only on a dare from my older brother. Let this serve as a warning. Do not try this at home (or the Laundromat). I still get a little woozy every time I think about doing laundry. "Nope, sorry honey, I wish I could help you with those dirty clothes, but you know I had that one bad dryer experience."

As I am finishing my hot dog at the turn, I am thinking about borrowing (stealing) the fan off the dashboard of the cart parked next to mine. I don't see anybody around & the owner likely partnered up with another golfer, left his cart here, and is obviously not using that fan. I could leave a note that says I will return it to the clubhouse after my round? No, I'd probably just get arrested. And Phoenix is not the place to spend any time in jail. Joe Arpaio has been the sheriff here since 1902 I think. I love this guy. His prisoners must wear pink jump suits and are fed calorie-correct meals that only cost 87 cents a day (Did you know that a bologna sandwich and apple sauce complete all your necessary dietary requirements?). The idiots at the state legislature demanded that cable TV be available to all inmates, so he complied but only shows history and cartoon channels. The prisoners, and before you start to feel sorry for them, they are criminals...work on cleaning up the Phoenix roadways during the day and sleep in tents in the desert heat at night. Don't want that lifestyle? Don't commit a crime in Maricopa County.

As we get ready to start on the back side, I stare down the 10th fairway and have high hopes of a better game than I played on the front. I also have high hopes the temperature will sneak back to double digits soon. July can't last forever and then comes August. Oh wait... that's when the monsoon season starts here. I suppose that's a misnomer. I'm not great at geography, but I'm pretty sure Phoenix is nowhere near Asia or the Indian Ocean. I do recall seeing a Thai restaurant on the way to the golf course. High winds and torrential rains do occur in the Southwest, but lasting only four or five minutes, they hardly qualify as monsoons, however; it does give the excited weathermen here a chance to use their colorful charts and graphs.

There's a job that must require a tremendous amount of talent, Phoenix TV meteorologist. It is the creative person who can come up with so many interesting ways to tell viewers that today (and every other day in the Valley) is going to have sunshine. Three hundred and seven; that's the number of days every year when there is more sunshine than not. The other fifty-eight days have more clouds than sun, and some rain on occasion, but only a total of seven inches annually. The weather events that are significant during August are the 'brown-outs'. These dust storms pop up out of nowhere and can be a mile high and several miles wide. With the high wind speeds, it passes quickly, but if out in it... you are sand-blind. A neighbor, who had nearly reached her home, was seen driving her convertible with the driver's door open, staring down at the curb to find her driveway during one of these dirty storms; dangerous and blizzard-like, but with hundred degree temps. But it's a dry heat.

Weddings and Funerals

There are momentous occasions that mark our existence on this planet, and I have found a mathematical average pertaining to two of these events. For every year you are alive, you will attend one wedding and one funeral. Sixty-two years old? That's sixty- two weddings and sixty-two funerals. I have studied this hypothesis and given the matter considerable attention. And I have made intensive inquiries in order to substantiate its validity. I worked on it for nearly a whole week and have accumulated data from high-ranking government officials (Bert has been with the post office for 31 years). There are a few professions that skew the average, so I've excluded funeral directors and clergy. And if you've been married more than once, the factor is multiplied by the number of times you've walked down the aisle. If you've died more than once, please contact Shirley MacLaine for more info.

The basis of this theory assumes that the older you get, the more people you come into contact with, thus the increased number of ceremonies to attend. For multiple marriages, you are exposed to all the events of both sides of several families. Good luck with that, by the way. My wife and I have each been married before and owned a business where weddings and wakes occasionally took place. It stands to reason our numbers may be slightly above this average; we are on a first-name-basis with all the funeral home directors. Humans have been trained early in their development to celebrate matrimony as a joyous occasion, and to dread the observance of a death as depressingly sad. As I get older, I am finding the emotional lines between weddings and funerals a wee bit blurry, and not sure whether it is apathy or the amount of alcohol required to get through either.

My wife and I recently attended a friend's daughter's wedding. It did not seem all that joyous, as the bride's estranged father and his new wife spent most of the evening arguing at the next table. I really wanted to enjoy the pulled pork dinner, but the pig was still doing most of the pulling. There was cake... just not enough of it. And while I normally embrace cultural differences when it comes to music genre, I insist that tasteless rap is just garbage with a beat. I offered my wife a new set of golf clubs if we could leave before 8:30.

On the other side (if you'll pardon the here-after reference), we went to a funeral Monday and the laughter that filled that church could be heard for blocks. I'm sure the family was devastated by the loss their beloved patriarch, but they chose to celebrate his life with the same playful banter that made him so popular. I liked that... and the booze served afterward... and the sleeve of golf balls each mourner got to take home. Now that's a funeral! If everybody I know would do that, I could save a bundle on my liquor tab and golf budget. Who do I see about getting Titleists next time?

Unfortunately, fewer weddings and more funerals will appear on our horizon as we mark off the years. My wife gets up early every day, races to the mailbox, and grabs the morning Times to view the obituary page before her first cup of coffee.

Hell, it takes me three cups of java to be convinced I've stayed out of that section of the paper for the day. She doesn't want to miss paying her respects to all the people we have met over the years. We could go to a visitation once a week if I owned more suits. Seeing me in the same blue blazer over and over has apparently caused some stir in our social circle. In the last two months alone we attended eleven funerals. Is this the life we thought we were missing out on by coming back to Iowa from Florida? The odds of us attending a funeral there were pretty slim, we only knew eleven people.

I always look forward to our social events of the upcoming weekend, unless of course there's a funeral to attend. But if there has to be death, let's hope they celebrate the life with an open bar and Titleist golf balls... I've got a tee time on Tuesday.

Purpose or Obsession

Finding purpose in retirement may be more about perception than reality. Take my neighbor Fred. He spends countless hours in his wood shop making toys for his church. The church then sends the toys to children in third-world countries. Everyone thinks Fred is a hero and I am personally in awe of his significant contribution to society, albeit perhaps a bit jealous. My wood-working skills are somewhat lacking, and unless these kids like to play with paper-weights or ashtrays... the church would likely seek a cease-and-desist order to discourage my efforts. But truth-be-told, Fred is cursed by his passion. He can't stop making the toys. He is fixated on this hobby. I have deduced, with my incredible knack for human nature and having a minor in psychology (okay, so it was one psychology class and yes, she was a minor but I didn't know that at the time)... that Fred is suffering from obsessive-compulsive behavior as a result of his guilt and anger over his wife's extravagant shopping benders.

Take Fred's wife (please-and-thank you, Mr. Youngman). She has no respect for the money he made during his working years, while she spent her days at the mall. And now, she sits on her fat assets and shops on-line 24/7. His 401K is rapidly becoming a 201K. She insists that shopping every day stimulates the economy, and her use of coupons saves them money that they would not have had without taking advantage of the bargains in the first place. So let's make sure we are all clear on this. She is saving them money by spending that money on things they don't need, just because of a discounted deal. That same rationale put our country 14 trillion dollars into debt, and has convinced me to purchase the Rosetta Stone Chinese language program. Apologies for any suggested bias toward women, as I know that all females are not shopaholics. However, Fred's wife would shop in her sleep if the QVC volume didn't keep the dog up all night. And while not necessarily a sign of genetic predisposition; her 10-year old granddaughter recently chronicled the top twenty department stores in her smartphone by GPS codes. She likes saving valuable time getting from sale to sale on bargain days. I am so thankful my wife does not fall into this category, and I feel sorry for my neighbor Fred.

Many passions and projects that require repetition become obsessions for all of us. For me, this behavior might rear its ugly head in the form of grass cutting. Hey, don't laugh. Men take this matter very seriously. We are taught at an early age to gauge our self-worth by the aesthetics of a perfectly-groomed lawn. The correct height of the cut, the straight lines and perfect angles, are all representative of our own abilities... and maybe virilities. Our feathers plume when we create the ultimate green masterpiece. We strut after every cut. And jealousy? I've seen grown men cry when a neighbor brings home a new zero-turn-radius John Deere rider. Where do you think the phrase "green with envy" comes from? Sod is God. Thou shalt not covet thy neighbor's yard.

My need for a perfect lawn came from watching my father

mow his yard. It was frightening. He would start on the perimeter and mow around in circles, throwing the grass toward
the center to be cut and re-cut, again and again. He would continue this pattern until the mower was choking and gagging,
trying desperately to get through the heavy clumps. He was not
actually cutting the grass so much, as beating it to death. I felt
sorry for that Briggs & Stratton motor and hope that someday
my nightmares eventually subside.

I've tried to explain the proper grass-cutting techniques to
my wife, but to no avail. Curvy lines for women are normally a
good thing, but not when it comes to lawns. After a recent stint
on our John Deere, the lines of her mown path looked as
though she had fallen asleep and veered off target... continu-
ously. She insisted the steering wheel should be looked at, and
made some comment about the need for a cup holder for her
lemonade. She only drinks lemonade when accompanied by
Smirnoff. I do not believe she is taking this seriously. It has
become necessary for me to ban her from all mowing and I
have hidden the key to the tractor. She complained a little at

first, but didn't actually seem all that upset by this exile. I only mention it, having just seen the note on the kitchen counter that reads: WENT SHOPPING...TOO MANY COUPONS IN THE PAPER TO PASS UP...LOVE YOU...ENJOY YOUR MOWING. Hmm. This might be a good time to go on-line and take a quick peek at our 401K.

Wear It with Pride

I can't quite put my finger on it, but the dress code for men over sixty these days,   looks more like 'unemployable' rather than 'retired-casual'. Yesterday, I slipped into a watering hole I used to frequent and at first, didn't recognize a soul. While it may have taken a while for my Transition Lenses to kick in, I was not prepared for what I eventually came to see. There were seven older men sitting at the bar talking and each said hello as I pulled up a stool. I noticed they were all considerably over-weight and slovenly in appearance, wearing dirty hats and torn jeans and t-shirts. Two had full beards and the others had apparently chosen not to shave recently. As I examined their faces one by one, I was surprised that I did know them; one lawyer, a stock broker, a couple of builders, and three teachers. Four had recently retired and the others were just practicing, I guess. I had not seen them for a few years. Where did the time go? And the dignity? By any measurable standard, they all ap-peared to have achieved slob status.

Having spent some time in Florida recently, I am accus-tomed to the many wardrobe malfunctions of the senior set there. Ranging from the curiously odd to the disgustingly re-vealing, my senses had been dulled by these sightings and I will never again be able to view the world as a reverent place. There were many times on the golf course where I was tempted to ask the guy in the cart with me, "Is your wife out of town... or has she died recently?" No way would my sweetheart let me out of the house looking like that. Thanks to the internet, we are all too aware of the fashionably-challenged gang that shops at Walmart. I realize this is a small group of people (they are people, aren't they?) who dress like this, and that it's a free country we live in. But it is painful for the rest of us to watch. Yet, we stop and stare anyway as if it was a decent car crash. At what point, as a society, did we become so frighteningly casual?

Men are supposed to age gracefully. Their graying hair is seen as a symbol of experience, knowledge, and conservative strength. That, in conjunction with the fact that women seldom have high expectations of us, should make aging a breeze. It must be tougher for women, however. They hold themselves to a higher standard and still adhere to the code that physical appearance is king (make that queen), and requires that they present themselves properly whenever in public. It's true some have to work a little harder than they used to, but the bright clothes, make-up, and perfume ensure their sags, bags, and smells remain camouflaged. Men tend to flaunt these flaws... or at the very least, ignore them. That may contribute to our female counterpart's woes. There is something to be said for diminished senses of sight and smell as we age.

I understand that natural progression must take its course. Our generation was cooped up in a suit and tie for 30 years, with women wearing dresses to vacuum the house. It makes good sense that we have moved the trend toward 'relaxed'. But we may have pushed the line a little too far. Our grandkids may see to it that casual Friday also takes place Monday through Thursday, assuming they will actually have to leave the house to go to work. If you don't have Skype, nobody cares what you look like when conducting business from the privacy of your home office. Pretty soon though, our younger generation's command of the English language will likely deteriorate to abbreviated text messages and Mr. Webster will be looking for a new job. " RU on face? Me2, bro." It is just a bit scary. And they complain when we groan and mumble. How is that different?

My wife arrived to meet me here for dinner at just the perfect time. I had just finished my pint and the last of the conversations with the 'old gang', and my hunger pangs were starting to kick in. As we headed toward the hostess stand, I overheard a young man in the foyer talking to his wife on the phone. "Yes dear, I'm here now and will get us a table. You wouldn't believe these eight old slobs I saw sitting at the bar..." What? There were only seven! I'll have you know this t-shirt I'm wearing was from the 1974 'Three Dog Night' concert, and you can't even see the holes in the underarm. And before it faded, it was a perfect color match to the coach's shorts I have on. And did you notice the blue stripes in the white socks? Oh yeah... exact same color as my Cubs hat... so don't even put me in the same category with them, you young punk.

My wife was squeezing my arm a little tighter now and pulling me toward the dining room. What's the rush, honey? The 'early-bird all-you-can-eat special' goes on for another hour or so.

You'll Wake Up One Day

I found myself sitting on a bench under the I-794 overpass, mesmerized by the lights and sounds of the trucks and buses as they sped by overhead. It was a beautiful fall evening, but the diesel fumes and the stench of stale beer had overtaken my senses, and I was in a trance. In that brief out-of-body moment, I was trying to figure out how I came to be in that place at that time in my life. There must be a good reason why I was sitting under this bridge in downtown Milwaukee. I was startled by the crowd of strangers that had begun to surround me. An older gentleman sporting a hat made of Guinness beer cans, sat down beside me, not something you see every day. His shirt read, "The liver is evil, it must be punished". And then the band started and it hit me... Irish Fest.

As part of my wife's retirement bucket-list, she had booked a bunch of rooms for a weekend of family bonding and rekindling of her Irish roots. We have the time to travel, and back in the Midwest now after our brief stint in Florida, it was not uncommon for my wife to find some event in dire need of our celebratory assistance. She was not about to let these poor people go to all that work and not show up to appreciate their efforts. Bless her little heart. Any venue within a five-hour drive, that was celebrating anything of historic importance, was fair game. We visited town bicentennials, fairs and parades, museums and art shows, all apparently to make up for those times in our life that we missed because of work. Now don't get me wrong, I was up for most of these events, although watching a woman use a loom to weave a rug as part of Heritage Days was not one of them. We saw a great air show with the Navy's Blue Angels, and an exciting finish to the LPGA's Solheim Cup, as the USA defeated their European counterparts in a come-from-behind victory. These events usually serve alcohol and I have never been opposed to trading green backs for beer cans, especially to support a cause. Pretty noble of me, huh? But this Irish celebration is one you must add to your list.

I'm not sure that four days is ample time to right all the injustices of the world, but the Irish certainly give it their level best on this weekend. Poor and oppressed for so many generations, these Gaelic folks with their deep-seated Catholic faith are the most kind and generous people you will ever meet. And they take every opportunity to celebrate their heritage, albeit a history of struggles to overcome much adversity. It is a proud badge of honor they carry throughout their lives, and my wife and her family wear the colors well. In line at the bar earlier, the shirt in front of me read, "You can't drink all day if you don't start in the morning". Noted. And in front of that young woman, another read, "I'll have what the gentleman on the floor is having". They are no doubt strengthened by this phenomenal sense of humor, likely brought on by the notion that what doesn't kill you, makes you funnier.

So I'm sitting on this bench waiting for my shopping wife to return, amid thousands of singing festival-goers weaving back and forth in a sea of green and white and orange. I look down the row to my left and what do I see? My mother-in-law is at the end of the bench, waving her green scarf with one hand while clinging to her walker with the other. She's belting out every word of, "A Nation Once Again", and in that moment I realize my reason for being. My life's purpose suddenly becomes so clear. I have been brought to this place with my group of people, no doubt as part of God's master plan, to insure that they all will be led safely back to the correct bus that takes them to the hotel... as soon as the music stops and the beer kegs are empty. I am filled with noble purpose.

Another Winter?

I grabbed a cup of coffee and headed out the front door to stroll the 125 yards down our driveway in pursuit of the newspaper. I know the exact distance, as it is a perfect pitching wedge for me from the house to the mailbox. The dents in the top of the box are proof of my accuracy and reminders not to hit golf balls at noon when the mail carrier is delivering. He still won't talk to me. You'd think he would be in awe of my ability to hit such a tiny red flag from that far away. Non-golfer, I guess.

The air was a little crisp this day, but after the sweltering heat of the summer it felt refreshing. The dogs were barking and running the perimeter of the property, their daily routine to announce to the 'critter world' that the sheriff and his posse were patrolling the grounds. Only when the acreage was cleared could they plop down under a shade tree and be lazy bums for the rest of the morning. I was distracted by the loud honking and splashing from the geese on our pond. This body of water is apparently a stop-over on the main north-south aviation route for Canadian Goose Air. It's a two-acre farm pond, elongated in shape, and surrounded by corn fields that offer wide-open approaches for uninterrupted landings.

Occasionally, there are even a few regional commuter ducks that wander into our airspace. They are safe here and not in fear of my dogs, as the two mutts never learned to swim, or fetch... or show any interest or appreciation for the life of leisure we provide them. Ingrates.

The honking was the start of the gaggle's ritual for take-off procedures, as they splashed their way onto the bank to begin the required line-up. No matter how many times I watch these creatures perform this innate ceremony, I am always amazed by the consistency in their actions before flying off. One-by-one, they find their place in line and wait patiently for the others to follow suit before the announcement to turn off all cell phones and pagers. I count thirty-two birds on this flight, and the occasional cackles heard are likely flight attendant instructions about the oxygen masks that may fall down over their beaks in an emergency. I feel like I'm at O'Hare on a Friday afternoon.

I'm not sure who is in charge of their travel plans, but I suppose any bird-brain knows to head south this time of year. And that's when it hit me. My mind began to wander and conjure up thoughts of snow and shoveling... and chest pains. Can I do another winter here? Sure today is nice, but the icy air that cuts through your lungs is only weeks away. I felt goose bumps (sorry) as the fear set in. Even though Florida didn't work out for us, I can't imagine staying here in Iowa for the duration of our golden years, having tasted a warmer climate. Maybe we shouldn't have been so quick to sell our second-home in Arizona when we moved to Florida. And why did we move back here again? I'm confused. Birds know instinctively that their survival depends on making the trek south this time of year. How do we humans not get that? I believe the survival of my sanity may be at stake if I stay here. I watch as the geese soar out of sight, and decide today will be the day I talk to my wife about the possibility of 'snowbirding' somewhere this winter. Back to Arizona maybe? I wonder how she'll react to that.

I am still leaning against the mailbox, mesmerized by the geese and my own thoughts of flying south, when the calm and quiet is interrupted by a golf ball that lands only a few feet away. And when another comes whizzing by my head, I snap out of my trance and realize my wife must be anxious for me to return with the newspaper. How long was I standing there in a daze? And more importantly, what club did she use to hit the ball 125 yards with such accuracy? Those were either two lucky shots or she's been practicing in secret, and I'm going to need a few more strokes from her on the course this afternoon. You don't suppose she was actually aiming to hit me, do you?

Let's Try This Again

When we first retired, I convinced my wife to follow me in the footsteps of my family. My grandparents retired and moved to Florida. My parents retired and moved to Florida. And in keeping with that Neanderthal tradition, off we went. But we never felt at home there, and once we realized that wasn't the place for us, moved back to Iowa. It didn't take that long. But now back in the Midwest, and facing the possibility of weathering another long, cold winter... I am totally freaking out. My thoughts lately have been of building a second home in Arizona, but my wife's thoughts have been more of, "How do I make my husband's murder look like a suicide?" She would like to stay in one place (apparently Iowa), and is not quite on the same page with me right now. Who can blame her? We've moved twice in the last year. Even I think I've lost the key to my roller skates.

As far as I can tell, you only go through life once, and if you are not moving then you are stationary. And if you are stationary, the dictionary defines it as "remaining in a single place"... a coffin for example. I may have paraphrased a bit. While I'm a big fan of silk pillows and the smell of fresh-cut pine, I'm not quite ready to crawl into that box for eternity. Thus, we need to be moving. As I'm explaining this theory to my wife, justifying my desire to go somewhere warm, I toss in the erroneous fact that a coffin's insulation R-factor is a negative number in the 'frozen tundra' of an Iowa burial plot. That coupled with the concept of a spring thaw disrupting the vault's seal (allowing water seepage and worms and bugs to creep in), pretty much made my case. My wife gave in and agreed to look at any Phoenix house plans that might arrive in the mail. Miraculously, several appeared next to her coffee cup on the table. After all our years together, I'm not completely convinced my 'coffin' argument persuaded her to consider a winter bungalow in the Southwest. It is more likely that she agreed to my request so that I would shut up and keep my senseless drivel to myself. That works for me.

As we discussed aloud the possibility of another move, those people closest to us were supportive ... once they stopped laughing. Their offers to help came in the form of phone numbers to well-respected local therapists. "Who moves from Iowa to Florida and back to Iowa in a year... and then goes to Arizona for six months?" I raised my hand. "No, we mean who else?" While another might have been influenced by their negative reaction, I was not dissuaded. Everyone is entitled to an opinion. My wife often gives me mine. I realize the cost associated with owning two homes is somewhat impractical, and the thought of house maintenance on two fronts sure seems daunting, but I still believe the pursuit of this goal is viable. If I'm not in Iowa in the winter time, what do I care if the driveway gets plowed? It will melt in the spring. And if I'm not in Arizona in the summer, what do I care if it's 118 degrees? No sweat, so to speak. My master plan is starting to come together.

We toyed with the idea of renting like many snowbirds do, but if I'm going to part with twelve thousand dollars, I'd rather fling it at a mortgage.   Besides, the major holidays (Thanksgiving, Christmas, and of course St. Patrick's Day) all fall during this period, and we're going to feel more 'at home' surrounded by our own stuff. The initial internet search of possible communities in the Phoenix area was narrowed by our list of criteria. The first and most important factor was cost, followed by a close second... which was also cost. After that, we wanted an age-restricted community on a golf course, with a pool and a big yard for our dogs. Is that too much to ask for a couple of spoiled retirees? I think not. I believe we found the perfect place in a western suburb of the Valley and hope to eventually call that 'home # 2'... again. It's okay, I get confused trying to keep it all straight, too. And you think this retirement thing is easy? I'm just keeping my fingers crossed that my wife won't swap this house for a different husband.

The Last Harvest

Good-bye Iowa, again? Actually it should be 'aloha', which means hello or good-bye, for those folks who can't make up their minds whether they're coming or going. In my case, it's about where we live. I'm ready to move somewhere else, or at least spend the next six months in Arizona for the winter. It's too cold here. My wife, on the other hand, has had enough of this 'state-hopping'. Iowa to Arizona, back to Iowa and to and from Florida. I can tell she's ready to call the 'wacko-wagon' and have me tossed into the hoosegow. When I was growing up, my Grandaddy always said to "follow the straight and narrow, boy, or you'll end up in the hoosegow". As a little kid I imagined this being a dark, far-away place, like Mr. Bockman's tool shed down the block. Later, in my teens, I figured he was probably talking about prison. But now I see he was warning me of a much scarier place... the marital 'dog house'. I know I've approached the 'squirrely gates' when my wife announces her frustration with me by saying, "I've got one nerve left and you're standing on it." I sense she would like me to forget about snowbirding in Arizona, and concentrate on making one place our home. I get that feeling because she used those exact words yesterday. I am so quick to catch on.

I read an article last week about life's four seasons, in which they compared the teenage years to the 'spring' season of your life. At this time you experience hope and young love and promises for a terrific future. Next you get married (so much for the hope and promises) and start a family and apparently enter the 'summer' season. There is baseball, soccer, swimming and cheerleading... and the kids have fun stuff they do, too. Next comes 'fall'. The children have left the nest and gone off into the world (where else would they go?). You supposedly find new hobbies and a renewed connection with your spouse, and love is all goo-goo-ga-ga again. It is possible my fall... fell. And then comes 'winter'. It's cold and you're old. Is it me, or does that just not sound like something to look forward to?

I personally sailed through 'spring' a little too quickly. 'Summer' was a hoot, except I broke my leg twice and never got to lead a cheer. 'Fall' really has been a good season for my wife and me, and we are closer and better connected. But that may have more to do with downsizing to a smaller space and co-dependence on a joint retirement account. So when does this 'winter' thing start, anyway? Am I going to hear sleigh bells ring? Odds are if there is a sleigh, then there is a horse. And if there is a horse, then I will likely have to clean up after him. I've never roasted a chestnut on an open fire in my life, and I understand that cold weather tends to shrink those up anyway. Sleet and snow and ice make me numb, and it is not possible to come up with anything remotely fun when you are numb. I don't ski, so don't even go down that run. The rational conclusion for anyone living in a northern zone, would be to drive to a warm southern zone as they get older. Do it now people before they take your keys away!

As I look up and stare at the silks playing peek-a-boo under the golden tassels (I'm standing in a cornfield at this moment, so all you guys reading this and picturing a centerfold, relax), there is a crispness to the fall air. It is comforting and refreshing, but a warning sign that winter is just around the corner. I tell my wife that this is a signal for us to take the six-month hiatus to milder temperatures. This 'fall' season of our lives has been so good to us, and we'll be able to stay in it longer if we go south now. We don't want the 'winter' season to enter the picture too quickly, right? Metaphors are fun.

I'm getting 'the look' as I try to get her to narrow down the floor-plan choices for our next Phoenix house. She's saying "maybe", but shaking her head from side-to-side. I take that as a definite yes. But I had better not push her too hard. The thought of 'being out in the cold' for a long period of time, reminds me... there are two people in this world that you don't want mad at you... and my wife is both of them.

Landscape Rocks!

The house construction is going according to schedule and it won't be long before we leave for Arizona and become snowbirds. The idea of summers in the Midwest and winters in the Southwest finally seems like the right combination for us. I can feel the cold of an Iowa winter approaching in the crisp air this morning. Over a cup of coffee, I was trying to remember why we sold the last house we owned in Phoenix so many years ago. Trying to maintain two houses and work full time was certainly a challenge. And we were hardly ever there, especially in the summer. Waaaaay tooooo hot! Maybe that was it. But, there must have been other reasons. It was such a cute little home situated on the old golf course. My wife had it decorated in a golf theme, and our neighbors to the west were so nice. Oh yeah, now I remember... the next door neighbor to the east was seriously creepy. This guy would stare at my wife all day long and make suggestive comments. Of course I do the same thing to her, but according to Playboy, it only becomes creepy when done by a neighbor. That situation, coupled with the buyer's offer of twice what we paid for the house... made our decision to sell pretty easy at the time. I am however, glad to be back in the same area and convinced our new lot is big enough, and the house angled in such a manner, as not to be bothered by any peeping Jacks (not to mention any names). That is of course, if anybody ever decides to build around us. We are on the new golf course now, but in such a remote area, we need a Garmin GPS and an extra tank of gasoline to get to the clubhouse. There are no other homes currently being built on this street. That's perfectly fine with me. I like open spaces and could live without talking to other people... ever.

Once the final walk-through and closing were completed, the property had to be landscaped within sixty days. There are a lot of dumb homeowner association rules regarding types of plants allowed and color choices of rock for the yard. Yes, rock. Because of Arizona's obvious water challenges, a restriction is placed on the amount of grass a homeowner can plant. Only 25% of a yard can be grass. And you'd have to water it twice a day and mow it twice a week to keep it looking nice in this heat. Enough said. I just became a big fan of rock. So I ordered the landscaper to top-dress the entire yard with brown rock once all the plants were in. I neglected to ask the price of said rock because, well... it's just rock. How much could it be, right? For the record, I am a moron. In case someone asks, I am as dumb as a dump truck. Yes, I have boulders for brains.

The row of semi trucks that brought the rock that afternoon stretched around the block. Apparently the rules require a minimum amount of this stuff per square foot, or cubic yard, or however much the contractor's brother-in-law needs to pay off his new Ford F-150 Super Cab. The last of the delivery drivers presented me with a ten thousand dollar invoice (holy $h*#) and I told him in no uncertain terms, "Listen Mac," hang on... here it comes..."You are completely 'stoned' if you think I'm gonna pay that much for a pile of crushed rock that's just going to sit around on the ground and serve absolutely no purpose."

He didn't argue the point with me, stuffed a customer-service number in my shirt pocket, and climbed into his rig and pulled away. I could have planted Zoysia grass and hired a live-in gardener for the next fifteen years for that much money. Did I mention I'm an idiot?

After I pay the rock bill, I won't be able to afford a drip-system for the new plants. Without water, they will turn brown and die. I could save a bundle and cancel the pool that my wife wants, but then she would shoot me and I would turn brown and die. If we're looking for an up side to these two options, the plants and I, if dead, would match the color of the yard rock perfectly. My wife suggested we could save some money by cancelling the stucco wall we have designed to fence in the entire property. But now more than ever, I think we'll need it to keep the thieves from stealing our newest, most valuable possession... the landscape rock.

Grand Design

I'm going to be late today. I just couldn't get everything done this morning before heading out the door to my golf lesson. It seems as though age plays a role in that process for most men. The older I get, the more obstinate my body becomes, and the more time it takes to get through the morning's requirements. I am thankful (on so many mornings) not to have been born a woman. In addition to waking up to a snoring and unshaven husband, I would need extra time to put on my make-up, shave my legs, and iron some clothes. I suppose a shower would also be a good idea.

My golf instructor lives on the other side of Phoenix and it takes about an hour to get there from my house. It would take longer in this city of a bazillion people were it not for the engineers that design the roadway grids here in Maricopa county. These guys are good! With the influx of a million snowbirds every winter, county road gurus stay ahead of the curve (that's funny) by creating the thoroughfares long before the traffic needs arise. They are building roads in places today where there are currently no people, in anticipation of future developments. Most cities wait until the traffic backups become pileups before creating alternate routes. Having been in long lines in cities where there are far less people, I am personally in awe. Apparently that is not the case for the gentleman in front of me. He is halfway out the window yelling at the woman in the car ahead of his. It does not appear to be an invitation to his block party this weekend.

Driving is mostly relaxing for me. I pass the time in deep thought and can usually sort out any personal issues while behind the wheel. I think more clearly. I always drive the speed limit and that annoys my wife to no end. It also annoys aggressive drivers as I am often greeted with honking horns and one-finger salutes. I like all kinds of music while driving (that's not true, you can keep the rap), but would rather listen to a ballgame or talk radio if on a long journey. As I watch the other cars weaving their way through this morning's commute, I am reminded of the 'grand design' of these highways and ponder that premise for mankind in general. There must be a plan for all us. And there must be an alternate route, clearly marked with big orange signs, should your original plan be detoured. I have not yet seen those signs.

Spiritually speaking, people of most faiths believe in a master plan and a master planner. I certainly do. But in the big scheme of things, I wonder why there continues to be world hunger and double-bogies? What was the point of inventing the game of golf, with the goal being to break par on every hole, and then making that goal an impossibility? If par is 'average', as defined in the dictionary, breaking par on every hole would yield a score of 18-under. That has never been accomplished in a single round by any amateur or professional. And I doubt that the average scores of all golfers combined, is anywhere near par. To say every hole is 'par-able' is pure fiction anyway. That same dictionary describes the word 'parable' as "...a narrative of imagined events". So there you go.

My lesson today will be the intricacies of hitting my ball out of sand traps. Who first thought it appropriate to put a hazard smack-dab in the middle of a fairway? It's a "fair way". Isn't that where you are supposed to hit the ball? How is that fair? Whenever I get in one of those traps, I hack around like I'm digging for clams. I might as well take a shovel and pail in with me; and for as long as I'm in there, maybe a magazine. I really should be asking my instructor for advice in avoiding sand traps rather than tips to get out of them. For $125 per hour, you'd think he'd have figured that out by now. What does he really know anyway? He lost his tour card. "Them that can't do... teach?" I've been paying him for the past seven weeks just to tell me, "This game is played on the 6-inch course between your ears." What, he's a comedian? It is becoming obvious to me that the sand is in my head, next to the rocks.

I jerked the wheel to the right, to the apparent surprise of the guy who was currently using that lane, and just made the exit ramp in time. "Yeah, yeah buddy... I already knew that about my mother." Golf lessons are not the answer for me. If I turn at the next light and cut through the parking lot, I'll end up at my therapist's office. For $125 an hour, I should be putting that money where it will do the most good.

Hiking Is Not for Everyone

My wife is not the pushy type. She will casually mention the inkling of an idea that may be on her mind, tossing it out to see if I pick up on it, then reel me in slowly until I'm pretty sure it was my idea, and I find myself begging her to do it. How does she do that? If I tried that with her, I would break my reel, damage my inkling, and end up just begging her to do it anyway. I sometimes feel like it's a gender thing and the female species is so much further advanced than their male counterparts. I tried once to use the bird analogy, as the male of the species is much prettier and confident as it shows off its plume. She responded by saying, "What's the big deal? The female bird got his attention, made him do a silly mating dance, and didn't even have to put on makeup!" It reminded me of a cartoon I saw as a teen. A young boy and girl, with their pants down, are participating in a show-and-tell. The proud little boy says, "But you don't have one of these." And the little girl says, "True. But with one of these, I can get as many of those as I want." Women rule.

So it was no surprise when my wife suggested an outing that was outside my purview. At some point in our retired married life, we agreed to a plan wherein we would try one new thing every month. Something exciting that we had never done before. Okay, eyes back up here... this is not about sex, it's about adventure, I think. I always get those two confused. Once we established certain non-life-threatening parameters, i.e. no skydiving, swimming with sharks, petting Bengal tigers at the zoo, or voting for left-wing liberals... we were ready to take on just about everything else. Or so I thought.

The total bill at the sporting goods store came to $1,073.00. That should have been an early indicator that this was not going to be a good idea. Two pairs of Columbia walking shorts: $88.00. A North Face backpack: $159.00. Two pairs of hiking boots: $234.00. Water-soaked sun hats: $60.00. Authentic Aborigine walking sticks: $175.00. A four-pack of knee-high hiking socks: $37.00. What? Snakes and scorpions don't attack you above the knee? And two Lands End all weather pullovers: $320.00. Whatever we are about to encounter on this hike, we will surely face it in ultimate style.

I didn't mind the drive to the foothills. Traffic was light that day, and the cool breeze and wispy clouds helped make the bright sun bearable. I was surprised that the trailhead (see? I've even got the vernacular down) was marked by only a single pole jammed in the ground, along with a few discarded gum wrappers at the start of a worn path. "Oh the many of our forefathers who have traveled this path before us, chewing their gum...." My wife cut me short and said, "Can the wise cracks and get in tune with nature. This walk up the mountain will be a spiritual awakening for us." And sure enough, there was awakening.

I had not completely understood the purpose of the walking stick; just seemed like something extra to carry. First thoughts were it might ward off the critters I envisioned crawling around, lying in wait to attack unsuspecting novices who were wandering aimlessly in awe of the blue sky and red rocks. This was to be my weapon? My wife wouldn't let me bring my more effective 44-Magnum to this little outing. She insisted it would scare off other hikers. And still, I see it as the appropriate choice. It didn't take long to for me to realize this stick was also a decent balancing rod. I avoided a steep fall on some loose gravel and was glad to have it in hand. But the real purpose the Aborigines had in mind for this wooden pole became obvious as we got further up the precipice. It was a teaching aid.

I could hear the laughing and screaming ahead of us and it was getting closer by the second. Teenagers had been to the peak and apparently found recreation in the form of smoke signals to the neighboring 'Doobie' tribe. One of the girls, 'Mary Jane' I think, was undoubtedly completing a school project that involved 'joint' participation from her fellow classmates. As they passed us and poked fun at our shiny new threads, the teaching stick came in handy as an instructional guide, thus restoring peace and tranquility to our path (and a new-found respect for elders), as our hiker friends quietly made their way back down to the gum wrappers.

If the end result of a hike is to look back at your accomplishment and feel an increased self-worth, then I guess it has its merits. Exercise? I have a treadmill that looks at a 46" plasma and together they cost less than my outfit. The following weekend we took a different path, but I still didn't get the attraction. I think I can say with some confidence, that these two hikes complete this bucket list item. It was difficult for me to find any value in this hobby, or is it called a sport? My wife proposed that climbing rocks and experiencing nature was supposed to be 'free entertainment'. But as it turned out, our cost-per-outing came to $536.50. The next time it's her turn to suggest a new adventure, I'm just going to give her $500.00 to go shopping... and save the $36.50 for my greens fees.

Out of the Pool

It would be difficult to live in Phoenix in the summer and not have access to a swimming pool. The 115 degree heat is stifling and a refreshing dip every afternoon seems an absolute necessity. Actually, the top five basic human needs for people living in the Southwest are in order: 1) water, 2) food, 3) aggressive driving skills, 4) a swimming pool, and 5) a bathing suit... to cover the unpleasantries of an aging anatomy. Nobody wants their skin and their eyeballs burned at the same time. The sun and sky and mountains are so breathtaking, you just have to be outside enjoying all that the Valley of the Sun offers, no matter what time of the year it is. So when it's too hot to golf, find the pool. I cannot remember a time in Iowa when it felt good to be out in the elements during the five frozen months of winter. Even if you like to snowmobile or ski the slopes, there is considerable danger involved when it is 25 degrees below zero with wind-chills of minus 40. I found that the best recourse was to slip into a tavern and hang out with some of my closest friends: Jim, Johnnie, and Jack. That would be Mr. Beam, Mr. Walker, and Mr. Daniels. Maybe that's why I don't remember.

And while having that pool in your backyard is great in the summer, the cost of trying to heat it during the winter is ridiculous. I remember a January when my wife's sister and her kids and grandkids all stayed at our house in Arizona. It was cooler than normal for that time of the year, with highs in the fifties. But the lows dipped below the freezing mark and the poor natives were comatose. We were in Iowa at the time and got a phone picture from them swimming in the steamy pool. My wife started crying at the photo of everyone splashing around and having fun, and was obviously missing a good time with her family. I wanted to feel sorry for her, but I too was wiping my eyes after seeing the photo. The average cost to heat that much pool water is about $600 per week, and the steam rising off the water looked to me like $20 bills wafting through the air. I couldn't go near any body of water for a week after getting that utility bill. I ended up considerably dehydrated and badly in need of a shower. That would explain the case of air freshener my wife left on my nightstand.

I have discovered however, that owning a pool can be very costly, even if you never turn the heater on. A pool service comes every Monday to check the p-H levels in the water. If the 'p' is for pool... what is the 'H' for... Herbicide? After a thorough scrubbing of the PebbleTec walls, our 'pool boy' whips out his little chemical kit; such a nice young man, attending Arizona State University, I think. A couple of drops of this and that, and shake with water... presto! You've got a hydro-sapphire martini. I bought a big, green, inflatable plastic olive that floats around in the pool all day. I don't fully understand photosynthesis, and I had to look up how to spell it, but apparently the hotter the air temperature, the quicker the water can become unstable. I had an ex-wife like that once. I saw what happens to a pool that is left unattended for a full month. A friend headed back to Portland one August, thinking his pool had enough stabilizer in it to endure the brutal heat. Upon his return, 'Larry' encountered a slimy, green Petri dish where the pool used to be, and the growing stuff was quickly taking over the back yard. He and his wife spent three days scouring the side walls after putting enough shock tablets in the water to disinfect a city dump site. After a recent pool party of theirs, I did notice how remarkably soft my skin was... and that I now glow in the presence of black light.

My wife is convinced the pool is worth the extra money for its maintenance. She says she cringes whenever hearing about the health risks of parasites that can live in warm, untreated water. I believe, on the other hand, that the warm-water 'parasite' is actually the pool boy. He never takes his eyes off my wife and I think she is enjoying the attention a little too much. She so looks forward to his weekly visits, and always seems to smell really good on those days... as I'm heading out the door for the tennis lessons she signed me up for on Mondays. I'm sure it's nothing.

Let's Volunteer

As a younger man, I always thought that I would volunteer more when I retired. I did find the time to serve on a number of charitable boards and give back to our community for much of my adult working life. But owning and managing a business took so much time and effort, it was difficult to participate often enough. Thankfully, there was no shortage of thoughtful strangers who would call every day to allow me the opportunity to donate my money and services to their fund-raising events. Bless their little hearts. I have sponsored runs, walks, crawls, golf outings and baseball innings. I have sold, bowled, and braved the cold for countless charities. And then there's my wife. We all feel rather insignificant when we try to measure up to her philanthropy. The hungry, homeless, and abused are in a better place thanks to her. And those are just the dogs; you should see the people she's helped. She's done more to raise money in this town than the city tax assessor. Eventually she started her own not-for-profit, put me to work as a volunteer of course, and enabled me to log more hours than Paul Bunyan. So when I finally retired and had more time to volunteer, I promised myself I would try to be more like my wife. That could be seen as an explanation for the night I tried on her pantyhose, tripped, and broke through the glass sliders onto the porch. Our guests were only slightly amused and never quite looked at me the same after that. Let's move on.

It has been fun to go to new places and meet new people who share the same passion for charity work. There is a common bond among volunteers and each has their own story behind their kindheartedness. You certainly get a great feeling when you see the good in other people and receive the thanks from those you help. But I am finding out there are too many great causes every weekend, and my golf pals are complaining that I am not contributing enough to their 'favorite charities'. I always lose at golf and there seems to be little doubt as to why I am their friend. "Friends don't let friends lose money to perfect strangers." My loss however, has been their wife's gain. I've paid for one hip, a set of collagen lips, and have full equity in approximately three and a half boobs. It annoys the men when I ask to look closely at where my assets have been placed.

On this month's upcoming volunteer list we have: 'Ride with Rob', 'Pamela's Poker Run', and the 'Pub Crawl for Paul'... you can't make this stuff up. We've already covered most cancers and a lot of capital letters: MS, ALS, and SSF. With all the exercise I've been getting, I should have shed a few pounds. But apparently that's not how it works. The after-event party for each of these worthy causes serves plenty of food and drink (so you can place inebriated bids on baskets of wine and chocolate). And being the full-blooded American that I am, this stuff is not going to go to waste. I think my net magnanimous expansion is now two full notches (on my belt), or the equivalent of about 20 pounds. Pretty soon the family will need to create a walk on my behalf titled, 'Move It for Mike' (because he can't). That being the case, my wife has insisted that cut-off tees and Spandex running shorts are no longer outerwear options for me when participating in these walks...or any actual walking "more than five yards beyond the front door of our house". Yep, that's a direct quote. And she muttered something about my body reminding her of a Weeble.

I don't know how I'll be able to break the promise I made to myself (really?) to be a better human being. No seriously, I need to serve the community in a greater capacity. I need to take on more events... okay, stop...I'm over it. I'll never be my wife. Now I just have to convince her that these benevolent causes are clogging up my golf calendar, not to mention my arteries. Maybe I could fake a knee injury at the next 5K race? Or throw my arm out while bidding on an auction item? No, that won't work. She'll see right through that. And knowing her, she might just host a post-marital fundraiser with her divorce attorney entitled, "Walk Out with Pat".

Distractions

Life is full of distractions. If everything always went as planned, we'd never be stuck in rush-hour traffic... and miss seeing the billboard that directed us to the realtor who would find us the house of our dreams. And there would not be long lines to stand in... and we'd miss the opportunity to strike up a conversation with the person we eventually married (except of course for the Department of Motor Vehicles, where there will always be long lines, designed to break you into submission). How boring would life be without adversity? Misfortune, and how you deal with it when it jumps in your path, determines the direction of that path on your journey in life. This is the conversation my wife and I had over coffee this morning.

We have always taken the first twenty minutes of every day, to discuss our 'life pro-forma'. It's our own all-encompassing personal balance sheet of sorts, wherein we analyze strategies for our physical, social, and financial well-being. Sounds like a pretty heavy way to start your day, but if you spend a few minutes daily to put your life in perspective, it never seems so daunting. Of late, our assessment has been as follows: a) physically, we are overweight and need to exercise more, b) our social status is non-existent since we retired and moved out of state... and back again, and c) our financial portfolio looks more like a scrap book. After the events of the last few months, where stocks tanked, the fraudulent credit-swap debacle was unveiled, and the housing market crashed, we found ourselves suffering many of the same ills that have plagued all Americans. Our retirement account has self-imploded.

So, like the many people who are hurting in this economy, we pulled ourselves up by our boot straps (okay, I honestly have no idea what a boot strap looks like... let's make that soft spikes)...and headed to the golf course to forget how miserable we are. We always enjoy the Arizona sun against the blue sky and the mountains, and can set any pace for our game as a twosome, since the course is seldom busy most mornings. We realize this visit is just a long vacation, and that we must squeeze every ounce out of it before heading back to the Midwest. And whatever happens over the course of the next few years in our life, we consider ourselves to be lucky to have experienced this retirement lifestyle, if even for a brief moment.

This particular day we would be paired with a very nice couple from California who were visiting relatives that lived in this snowbird community. We spent most of the early holes trading questions about kids and jobs and hometowns, but noticed an odd occurrence when either of them would miss a putt on the green. They would call out a word, and then re-putt. Each time it happened, my wife and I traded puzzled expressions. By the time we finished the front nine, I felt compelled to ask. He explained that if he or his wife were distracted by any noises when striking the ball, they allowed themselves the chance to rehit with no penalty. "If a bird begins squawking in my backswing, I say 'bird' and take a mulligan. If a plane flies overhead, my wife can yell out 'plane' and take a mulligan." (I'm guessing Southern California?) First of all folks, this is a golf course with lakes and ponds, full of birds and geese. An occasional giggle from the gaggle is common and expected here. Deal with it and move on. And with an Air Force base nearby, take-offs and landings may also be considered an on-going distraction to the game, but are by no means, seen as handicap adjusters. We had made a friendly wager with these people at the start of the round, and were not particularly happy with their scoring methods. With our competition's use of mulligans, my wife and I obviously lost the $2 bet. Which, after the recent turn of financial events, seemed like $4. Unfair? Absolutely. Their distractions became our distraction. And so goes life.

While an early retirement seemed like the grand plan that would see us through our golden years, life had a different agenda for my wife and me. It is likely jobs will once again be in our near future, based on the way things are going. I suppose if we all got it right the first time, there wouldn't be a need for second chances. Thus the name of one of our dogs, Second Chance. I am glad that my wife and I got to experience the retirement lifestyles of Florida and Arizona, even if those events led us back to Iowa. We met wonderful people and discovered new and exciting things about ourselves and other cultures. And the return to Iowa gave us two of the best 'rescue dogs' we could ever have, so we are grateful (I'm not sure who rescued who). While we haven't yet decided on our ultimate Utopia, we look forward to the opportunity to react to future adversity and distraction as it comes our way.

Currently Arizona feels pretty darn good, especially since I stole a sleeve of golf balls off of Mr. California's cart while my wife was distracting him with her good-bye hug. I consider that appropriate compensation for the money we lost to those cheaters, and an opportunity for him to experience the broader gift of adversity in his life. Nice diversion, honey. Don't you just love distractions?

Holidays

Over coffee this morning, my wife and I were debating the popularity of all American holidays, ranking them in order of most favorite to least. I believe Christmas would top most lists, followed by Thanksgiving, followed by Mother-in-Law Day... I'm just trying to kiss and make up after rankling my wife's mom yesterday. She is spending a few months with us in Arizona. She lost her car keys again and wanted the spare set I keep with me. This is a fairly usual occurrence, and becomes a challenge when I'm so busy keeping important appointments half-way across town. Okay, so I was playing golf. Hey, it was important to me! And I didn't think it was a big deal, asking her to wait until I finished out the nine to come to her rescue. Now this is where we differ on what is considered socially responsible behavior. When she called, I was on the fourth hole. The nine I intended to finish out was the back-nine, of course. She knows I never just play nine holes. What would be the point in that? And it's not like I could just drop my clubs in the middle of the fairway, go let her in her car, drive all the way back to the golf course and say, "Excuse me, I was ahead of your four-some but had to go see my wife's Mommy." She is not currently talking to me. Where was I? Oh yeah, holidays.

I remember the excitement of presents under the Christmas tree as a kid. And I loved the four-day weekends of turkey and football when I was a working adult. And now retired to a warmer climate, I get to enjoy playing the game of golf on all major holidays. There is a smell in the air at our course on these special days. It might be pies cooling on the window sill. No, I don't think people do that anymore. They're already at room temperature when you pick them up at the grocery. Perhaps it's the turf fertilizer being met with the early morning dew on our lush fairways? Maybe. But it's more likely just the sewage treatment facility being overwhelmed by the addition of all those relatives visiting our community this time of year. Whatever senses are being triggered, they are certainly not my imagination. There is no mistaking the feeling you get sneaking in 18 holes while the rest of the world sleeps in, or prepares for the onslaught of in-laws. My little endorphins jump around and bump into each other and that's better than a sugar high.

I don't necessarily score any better on holidays. Eyes up here... I'm still talking about golf. It may be that I am distracted by my excitement or just by the solitude. There are seldom other golfers in sight, especially on Christmas morning. Most of the residents here are entertaining their grandkids or sucking down enough Bloody Marys to get through the yelling and the screaming. And that's from the family members without kids. There is certainly nothing more satisfying than reaching a par-five in two shots, making the putt, and then calling a close friend to tell him about the Christmas gift you just got on the last hole. Especially if that friend lives in Minnesota. While possibly happy that I made the eagle, said friend is never happy to hear that I'm enjoying golf in 65 degrees, on a sunny day in December. And isn't that why you call? If you can't make a friend jealous, who then? Your enemies don't care and families never harbor any envy. They already know when your bucket gets tipped over, they stand to inherit the golf cart AND the house on the fourth green.

I remember getting those Christmas calls from friends who retired before me. For the record, they are older than I am and I never miss an opportunity to remind them of that fact. Whether in Florida, Arizona, or Southern California, I always thought it was nice they would stop to call me in the middle of a busy round. Trust me, with their struggling games... I'm sure they were busy. We would laugh that it was fifteen below in Iowa with the wind chill, and that Christmas for me would involve clearing the snow from the walks before the family showed up. I made sure to sound enthusiastic and envious, and so pleased they had been blessed with such good fortune and warm weather. However, my wife will attest that immediately after each of those calls, my phone would end up in the drapes across the living room. There was no more laughing. The last thing I wanted at Christmas was to hear from some schmuck on a golf course.

So on this holiday season, I am thankful for IPhones and a 4G network. I have a full compliment of friends' contacts so I can text, tweet, or email from any of our three golf courses... to any state with temperatures below freezing. That's good 'cause I know these folks won't actually answer a 'live' call from me.

Paws That Refresh

A national study was conducted and it was found that people live longer when accompanied by a pet. It is my understanding there is some emotional bond or sentimental tie that's supposed to make that statement true, but anyone with a dog knows other key factors actually come into play. Humans with pets will live longer because they can unwittingly force you to become physically stronger.

1 - *You get more exercise.* I have chased my dogs around the yard, up the driveway, off the couch, and in pursuit of Mr. Rabbit, Mr. Skunk, and Mr. Thompsen, the mailman. Apologies to the US Postal Service, but this story is about Mr. Squirrel. I was working in my basement shop and heard a screeching howl that could only come from my little warrior spaniel, Chance. Twice around the house we go until the squirrel she is pursuing flies up on to the stone above the front door. This dog is half way up the wall and neither of us is sure what she will hold onto when she gets higher. We're all three out of breath, and two of us are concerned for the safety of the squirrel. In my right hand I've got a garden hose trained on the little varmint, and my left hand is holding the dog collar, barely. My eyes however, were on the prospective buyers

heading up the driveway with our realtor. I'm sure that this first impression was not easily overlooked in consideration of whether or not to live at this zoo. The squirrel lived to tell his bushy tale, and Chance was napping it off ten minutes later. But, there was no offer made on the house that day. Go figure.

2 - *You increase your strength conditioning.* Ever try to get a chew toy away from a Labrador retriever? Not a smart move. Once my dog locks on, there is no getting back whatever it was that you were stupid enough to give him. You being me, of course, and me being stupid. This was a pull ring made of hard plastic and twisted rope. I teased him with it for ten minutes but never let him latch on. When he became disinterested, I slid it over my foot, sort of like an ankle bracelet, and sat down on the porch. A few seconds later, the ring is in his mouth, and I am upside down in the knock-out roses at the bottom of the steps. The flower's name is appropriate. I came to about 5 minutes later.

3 - *Your heart gets more adrenaline.* This hormone affects blood circulation and is good for you (in small amounts). From the kitchen, I could hear our fearless Westie barking intensely outside. She undoubtedly found an intruder in our yard, but the sound was faint and muffled so I went to investigate. 'Molly' was under the deck in front of our house and I could see the hole she had dug under the main beam. The deck sits practically on the ground, with a maze of 2x12's supporting the deck boards. She had apparently gone in after whatever went in ahead of her, and was unable to re-trace her steps. Her high-pitched squeal had captured my wife's attention by now, and there was some similarity between the shrill screams coming from each of them. It was heart-breaking to think Molly was stuck and scared. After a half hour of trying to coax her back out the only hole, I headed to the garage for my circular saw. I would cut a hole in the top of the deck closest to her last known location. My wife was yelling for me to stop, but I was pretty sure I had set the depth of the blade so as not to amputate any dog parts. There was an anxious silence for three or four minutes after the squealing had finally stopped. My wife and I just stared at each other. Within seconds, Molly sauntered out of the original hole with a mouse in her mouth. She was never scared, just on a mission. The piece-meal deck boards still give way a little when you walk on them. But the weather-resistant outdoor rug hides any evidence of the near catastrophe of that day. Not of Molly's adventure, but of my wife's threats to use that saw on me.

4-*You spend more quality time with your physician.* It was rare to get a glimpse of the coyote that had been stalking the creek bank just west of our house for the past three years. And while no Indian guide, I have seen enough John Wayne westerns to fake my way through a good set of tracks in the snow. With evidence of several small animals who had met their maker this winter, I was on the lookout to protect my dogs from a similar fate. This day, I let the dogs out the front door but forgot to search out back, and headed through the living room toward the back porch. He was just standing there. Our eyes met. Any shred of rational thought was lost in the moments that followed, as I grabbed the shotgun from the rack and burst into the ten-degree air. With no coat, no shoes, and no brains, the first set of icy steps seemed to offer little resistance. The stone fountain at the bottom of those steps however, did bring me to an abrupt stop... face-down in the snow. The gun went off, the coyote went off, and my lovely wife went off, when she came out to investigate the gunshot. The only fearful animal that day was the husband. I did say dogs are good for your health, right?

Eat, Play, Love

I have come to the place in this book where I need to get serious for a moment. Okay, I'm kidding. I do need to share with you though, that the journey through retirement would be impossible to bear if not for the love and support of your partner in life... and maybe a sense of humor. For me it's my wife. I can't actually say that out loud because she would start looking for a new home for me, like an asylum. Do they still make asylums? Like most men, I let on that it is somewhat tolerable having her around and that I appreciate that I don't dislike her most of the time. If you come right out and tell a woman that you are madly in love with her, and that you hang on her every word... you sir, will get dumped at some point. Women have innately been charged with 'fixing' men. And if you do everything they expect there will be no challenge. Boredom sets in soon after and you're tossed out like bad sushi. I don't really need to enlighten men about this phenomenon, as it is nearly impossible for us to act like that anyway. The only thing we truly fall for is an all-you-can-eat buffet.

"The way to a man's heart is through his stomach." That phrase is not just a wife's-tale, but the premise on which relationships have been built for centuries. Studies have shown that men think about sex seven minutes out of every waking hour. Food takes up the other 53 minutes. If we weren't worried about becoming physically unable to get up off the couch and walk to the dinner table, we'd eat ourselves motionless. And that obsession with food is magnified once you retire. Your libido may decrease, but your appetite becomes the number one factor in planning your day. I may still think about sex every seven minutes, but three of those minutes are spent trying to remember why. The rest of the time I say things like, "Well, after breakfast I'll clean the gutters." Or, "As soon as lunch is over, I'll wash the car." And, "Thanks for dinner honey, what's for dessert?" Never, ever underestimate how much we love food.

Playtime is also important in a marriage, too. And yes, I was thinking about sex when I said that, but I'm over it now. Sharing a common hobby is a great way to maintain a healthy relationship when you retire. You and she are going to spend a lot of time together. Minutes will become hours... and turn into days... and freakin' weeks, my friend! You better have a game plan for those times when your endearing charm and wit have run their course. Golf is the passion my wife and I have enjoyed for so many years. I taught her to play the game after we were first married, and about half the time now, she teaches me why that was a mistake. Just kidding. It is incredibly frustrating for the teacher to lose to the student so often. I am happy her game has progressed to a satisfying level (for which I take full credit), but still tease her that the wins only reflect her playing half the course when teed up from the forward markers. We have loved the times spent together on beautiful golf courses all over this great country, and were fortunate to have found a pastime so enjoyable. I love playing golf. There's that word again, love.

So eat, play, and love... the big three. You can decide in which order you prefer to list these secrets for a contented life. Women might argue that love should be listed first, and many popular songs have been written to support that stance. Men might list love third, but I don't recall any songs involving eating or playing (or playing with your food). I don't know if love really makes the world 'go round', but I can attest that eating too much makes my waist 'go round'. And if you get caught 'playing around' (there's that sex again), you lose the love and can't afford to eat after the lawyer takes his cut. So maybe we had better put loving first, eating second, and playing third. "Who's on first?" So here goes. I love (1)... to eat (2)... chicken wings after eighteen holes of play (3). You will never hear me say I rank food or golf above love... at least not out loud.

Identity Crisis

As I look back over the decisions I made in my life, I remember the day I told my wife I wanted to give up my good job as a restaurant manager and open an Irish pub. We had been married for exactly one year. She was not surprised, as it had always been a dream of mine to own and operate my own business, but had to wonder what she had gotten herself into marrying me. And in hindsight, while only thirty years old, with a new wife and a mortgage at 11% (the early 80's were brutal), it was possible that my timing may not have been the best. But, my wife says I get this look on my face when I focus on a project, that screams, "I am onto something here. Get out of my way." It should be noted that she too has a focused, recognizable look, one that I've seen many times over the years that says, "You're a moron". And then I just get out of her way. In this instance however, she was fully supportive and agreed to deplete our paltry savings and begin our successful 18-year journey as pub-partners. There may have been doubts along the way, but we never waivered in our commitment to this venture.

When the opportunity to sell the business came to us, we didn't hesitate at the chance to take an early retirement. We discussed the options, looked at our life pro-forma, and set a course. Any doubts were overshadowed by our resolve to make it work, no matter what. It has always been like that for us. We know what we want to accomplish and look forward to the challenges that come with the necessary dedication. And as a man, there is probably some innate force driving my need to provide a good life for my family. "Man bring home bacon - wife fry in big skillet". Whoa... and man ducks the big skillet! It was just a metaphor, honey. Step away from the pot rack.

There is this sense of calm I get when I choose a path to follow and have the confidence in my abilities to assess a situation, prescribe a game plan, and execute that plan with precision logistics. Throughout my adult life, I could see this path clearly everyday... until today. A fog has set in. No, better yet, a white-out blizzard of epic proportion has descended on my little path. I have not only hit a brick wall, I've mowed down the entire house and am headed for the neighbor's rose bushes. What happened? I feel shell-shocked. I lost ME. Yes, of course I looked in the last place I left ME, and I am not there. I've called everybody I can think of, but nobody has seen ME. Where did I go? Is this a mid-life crisis? No, maybe a little late for that. I have dropped my compass, though. And just for the record, I am apparently not good at being directionless. My dinghy has lost its rudder. The GPS voice on my Garmin is annoyingly repetitive... "Re-calculating, re-calculating." Maybe it's not "where is ME," but... "who is ME?" My only recourse is to re-trace my steps since I began this retirement saga.

Shortly after my wife and I retired, we moved to Florida. Is that when the train jumped off the track? There was a train? I don't remember any train. We drove, I think. Other than the really cool trams at Disney World, I cannot recall seeing any trains in my time there. That's odd. History books are full of accounts and references to Henry Flagler, a train mogul from Florida who has a county named after him. But he must have hidden them pretty well, 'cause the closest thing I saw resembling a train was a Congo-line at an all-inclusive resort in Miami once. Florida is a great place, but there just wasn't the fulfillment we were looking for.

Okay, next we moved back to Iowa. Why did we do that again? Did we take the train? There was this terrible winter, with snow and ice and wind chills that dipped below minus-thirty... for two months solid. Then we went to Arizona where there was no snow, no ice, and wind chills that hovered around plus-seventy. Then we came back to Iowa and the cold once more. That's it! All this freezing and thawing must have cracked my personal foundation. My wife insists that probably happened quite a few years back, but I believe it is recent. And with uneven footings, nothing I build on top of those basic blocks will ever be on the level, so to speak. I am of course talking about my identity here. I am still the same person I was, just not in pursuit of the same goals. If I want to be fulfilled, I'm going to have to change the way I think.

I followed my dream and then I sold my dream and forgot to get another. Where do they sell those? I thought retirement was going to be my next dream, but that's only a state of job-status. 'Not-working' is not a passion. And while I'm passionate about the game of golf, it is just a game... one that I'll never be able to master. I need to find a purpose-oriented project to wrap my head around, and start down a new path of inspiration. As soon as spring comes, I am going to repair my foundation and start building the next chapter in my life. Maybe I'll write a book.

The Book of Life Is Just a Rough Draft

As I approach the final days of my first two years in retirement, I look back and ask, "What the hell is wrong with me?" After completing such a long stretch of sound decision-making in my early adult years, how could I have mismanaged such a short period of time in my life? And at an age when I should have had it all figured out. There was a plan. It was a good plan. I deviated from the plan. I am a moron.

Life is like that, a deviation from the expected. It would not have been possible for you to disappoint your parents, had you done everything according to their plans. Where is the fun in that? And I'm sure after marrying Sally, you'd like to take a mulligan for that tattoo of "BARB" on your butt, but how boring would after-prom have been then? We are creatures of habit, but take great pride in our periods of non-conformity. Our nature is such that deviation from the norm, becomes the norm. Glass ceilings are made out of glass so they can be broken, right? Go outside the box. Try even if it brings you failure. Without failure, when would we know that we have achieved success?

Every day we're on this earth prepares us for the next disaster we get to become a part of. For me, that beats the pants off of knowing how things will turn out. For instance, do you really want to know when you will die? Can you imagine life as a countdown to the day and hour and minute of your demise? The angst would drive a boomer like me insane, and that would be a fate much worse than death. "Hey Paul... we're going to get in 18 holes this morning, grab a bite at the clubhouse, and then I've got to get back home and fall dead on the kitchen floor according to the plan. OK?"

It does take a plan to get to retirement, but with the volatility of the stock market these days, we've seen those plans can go awry. But the process of retirement is a gradual evolution of your dreams and wishes and cannot purely be defined by a plan. You may know how long you will work in this life, but you have no idea how long you are going to live. You may decide to end up near an ocean, but you will not just sit in your beach chair all day and watch the world go sailing by. Things change. Be prepared to accept those changes. You've heard the adage, "Plan your work, then work your plan." Good advice. Well, consider another one: "Plan to retire, but be ready to retire your plan", especially when it doesn't work out according to schedule. And remember, "The road to retirement is paved with good intentions." Mine was apparently a dirt road.

Ok, just a few more sayings and I'll let you go try retirement for yourself. "Swing for the fences." "Let the big dog eat." "Throw the Hail Mary". And if it turns out to be a bunt, or a shank, or an interception... you were a success because you had some skin in the game.   Pace yourself when your day to retire comes. It takes time to get it right. The only mistake you can make is staying on the bench. Along the way, you will be faced with many trials and tribulations (I had to look up that word - it means 'affliction'... then I had to look that word up - and it means 'misfortune'- I fully understand that word).   It isn't likely you were lucky enough to land your dream job on your first interview. Or that you married the first person you ever kissed, right? Oh, you did? That's a shame. No, I mean... I'm very sorry. No, really. I'm sure the two of you will be very happy, probably.

Most people have to take a second or third stab at something before they get it right. I thought I had my retirement all figured out, but I flailed around and bungled it. What I did finally come to see is that retirement is a moving target. You may take aim, but without adjustment to the 'scope', you could overshoot. I overshot. Thankfully I can re-load.

I might want to reword all this talk of stabbing and shooting, so as not to give any ideas to those I have made fun of in this book. Good luck in your retirement...I'm off to check my life insurance policies.

The End? (I hate that phrase)

Boomer Bungle

Made in the USA
Charleston, SC
15 July 2012